**THE PARK
LEARNING CENTRE**
The Park, Cheltenham
Gloucestershire GL50 2RH
Telephone: 01242 714333

UNIVERSITY OF
GLOUCESTERSHIRE
at Cheltenham and Gloucester

WEEK LOAN

657 4/2011

Club Cultures and Female Subjectivity

Club Cultures and Female Subjectivity

The Move from Home to House

Maria Pini
Research Fellow
Centre for Critical Psychology
University of Western Sydney
Kingswood, NSW
Australia

PARK LEARNING CENTRE
UNIVERSITY OF GLOUCESTERSHIRE
PO Box 220, The Park
Cheltenham GL50 2RH
Tel: 01242 714333

First published 2001 by
PALGRAVE
Houndmills, Basingstoke, Hampshire RG21 6XS and
175 Fifth Avenue, New York, N. Y. 10010
Companies and representatives throughout the world

PALGRAVE is the new global academic imprint of
St. Martin's Press LLC Scholarly and Reference Division and
Palgrave Publishers Ltd (formerly Macmillan Press Ltd).

ISBN 0–333–94606–5

This book is printed on paper suitable for recycling and
made from fully managed and sustained forest sources.

A catalogue record for this book is available
from the British Library.

Library of Congress Cataloging-in-Publication Data
Pini, Maria, 1965–
     Club cultures and female subjectivity : the move from
     home to house / Maria Pini.
          p. cm.
     Includes bibliographical references and index.
     ISBN 0–333–94606–5
     1. Women—Social conditions. 2. Women—Social life and
     customs. 3. Discotheques—Social aspects. 4. Rave culture.
     5. Femininity. 6. Sex role. I. Title.
     HQ1154 .P58 2001
     305.42—dc21
                                                      2001021723

10   9   8   7   6   5   4   3   2   1
10   09   08   07   06   05   04   03   02   01

Printed and bound in Great Britain by
Antony Rowe Ltd, Chippenham, Wiltshire

This book is for Maya

Contents

Acknowledgements

The work presented here, is in large part, the product of research conducted for a PhD thesis undertaken at Goldsmiths College. This research was funded by the ESRC, whose support I want to acknowledge with gratitude. The thesis was supervised by Professor Valerie Walkerdine, a great source of encouragement and support. I thank Valerie for her advice, her comments, her ideas and for her friendship throughout and beyond this research. Before starting the thesis, I had the fortune of being supervised by Angela McRobbie for an MA dissertation which I carried out on women and the early British rave scene. The PhD thesis would never have started without her support and enthusiasm and if I had not been so persuaded, inspired and moved by all of her very important work.

I thank the following for stimulating discussion and for offering useful feedback during my PhD research: Janice Cheddie, Andy Goffey, Dave Hesmondhalgh, Paul Pini, Hillegonda Rietveld and Tiziana Terranova. And I extend all my thanks to the different women who volunteered for interview. I spent some of the very best times of this research period conducting these interviews, and simply sitting and listening to the stories of these raving women.

My gratitude and love go to Tony for showing me that men can have as much fun out of raving as women. (Honestly, I didn't know this before!) Most importantly, for the initial inspiration, for fun, laughs, support and for the many good times we spent together, I want to thank Agi, Sybil and Rita, women who all contest the limits of appropriate or prescribed femininity, and women who have all found a 'home' on the social dance floor.

Material contained within Chapters 4 and 5 has been previously published within different edited collections. A version of Chapter 4 was published as 'Cyborgs, Nomads and the Raving Feminine' in Thomas, H. (ed.), *Dance in the City* (Macmillan, 1997). A version of Chapter 5 appeared as 'Peak Practices: the Production and Regulation of Ecstatic Bodies' in Wood, J. (ed.), *The Virtual Embodied: Presence, Practice, Technology* (Routledge, 1998). I thank both publishers for their useful feedback and comments.

Introduction

Raving, it's a different world. It *is* like a different world. It's like having a holiday, like having a month's holiday in a night and taking that month break in a night. (Teresa)

[Raving] is utterly different from everything else. It's a completely different world. It's like nothing else. (Clare)

The [rave] scene was like a whole society – a different society. (Miriam)

[Raving] is about letting go of being conformist, and being professional and proper and together. It's other to presenting that face of you. It's not necessarily the dark side of you. But it's the messy side of you. (Jane)

We all have images and dreams of an 'elsewhere' – landscapes which are both materially 'real' and imagined, and which afford some sense of release from, or alternative to, the mundane, the everyday or the difficult. These landscapes can be places of better material conditions, but they don't have to be. They can simply be places which suggest the possibilities for movement beyond the constraints, boundaries and regulations involved in everyday being – in being a woman, a worker, a mother, or a 'rational' subject for example. As Susan McClary quite rightly notes:

The musical power of the disenfranchised – whether youth, the underclass, ethnic minorities, women or gay people – more often resides in their ability to articulate different ways of construing the body, ways that bring along in their wake the potential for different experiential worlds. (1994, p. 34)

Whatever their make-up, these worlds or landscapes speak of alternatives to the conditions and possibilities which surround us on a day-to-day basis. They hold the promise of something *more*, or suggest something *beyond* that which is immediately attainable. In such spaces lies the potential for re-figurations of the here and now, the possibilities for creating alternative fictions or narratives of being, and the opportunities for the development of new (albeit temporary, incomplete and constituted partly in fantasy) 'identities'. As Stuart Hall puts it, identities:

> arise from the narrativization of the self, but the necessarily fictional nature of this process in no way undermines its discursive, material or political effectivity, even if the belongingness, the 'suturing into the story' through which identities arise is, partly, in the imaginary (as well as the symbolic) and therefore, always, partly constructed in fantasy, or at least within a fantasmatic field. (1996, p. 4)

Club Cultures and Female Subjectivity explores some such 'elsewheres' and (what are in some ways, very new) senses of belongingness. It is an examination of contemporary British rave and club cultures and its central focus is upon the modes of femininity which are being lived, figured and otherwise constituted in relation to these cultures. To put this another way, it is about women's suturing into the stories opened up by, and generated around, today's club cultures and the significance of club cultural belongingness for contemporary articulations of femininity. The book is the product of over eight years' research with women who regularly club and rave in and around London, and who claim that rave culture is central to their lives and to their identities.[1] The analysis which it presents is woven around the experiential accounts of 18 such women – all of whom were interviewed over this period (nine individually and eight within focus groups of two or three), and four of whom are quoted above. These women were aged between 19 and 35 at the time of interview, so this is not a 'youth' cultural study and this is centrally significant. Many of these women fall instead, within the recently popularised category of the 'thirty-something'. Such women have most usually been studied in relation to 'in home' activities such as television viewing and romance reading.[2] Part of this study's significance then, is that it touches upon the recreational practices of women who have traditionally been thought of in relation to a domestic context. The growing presence of such women within the world of House-parties, techno-music clubs and raves, is testament to the changing social structure within which we are living – a situation within which femininity's traditional 'life course' and its 'rightful place are shifting. *Club Cultures and Female Subjectivity* examines the role that social dance scenes can come to play within these changing times.

But why a study of femininity focused around nightclubs? The initial motivation underpinning the research was to make sense of the familiar claims being made in the late 1980s by female ravers and clubbers, that contemporary social dance cultures offered them access to a different 'world': a world within which lay the possibilities for the living out of alternative and more 'liberating' versions of femininity (Pini, 1997a). Ten years later, and although British rave has grown and diversified, claims such as the following remain familiar:

> [Raving's] about the time that you spend doing things that are about freedom. It's the time when maybe you can be yourself. Here's your normal everyday life, but going to a club or a rave is about something extra. (Jane)

> You just feel so free when you're raving. It is like pure freedom. (Teresa)

> [Raving's] totally about *me* and about what *I* want. It's my switch-off, my kind of get-out. It's when I think about *me* and what *I* want. (Catherine)

My aim at the start of this research was then, to make sense of why raving was considered 'liberating' by women such as the above. And I wanted to examine why the act of raving was constructed by many of these women as a kind of 'declaration of independence' as this is described by Janice Radway (1984) in relation to the practices of the Smithton romance-readers that she studied.

Although I have now been involved in this area of research for almost a decade, my interest has not waned. If anything, it has intensified over this period. This is partly because as a feminist living through what many see as a 'crisis' within feminism, I have become keen to explore popular articulations of so-called post-feminism. The contemporary social dance floor constitutes, it has been claimed, a particularly significant site for such manifestations (Bradby, 1993). My investment in this area has also grown because in thinking about the relations between popular cultural practice and the constitution of sexed subjectivity, I have come to revisit my *own* past and reflect upon various aspects of my *own* relations to femininity. Clubbing, partying and raving have, in many ways, been fundamental to these relations – impacting upon my experiences of aging, my relationships with others and my interest in questions about the 'rightful' place of women.

Something else however, has been *the* most important motor in driving my commitment to this research project, and in determining the shape of the current analysis. More powerful than a feminist interest in popular culture, or the results of a self-reflection upon my own transition from 'youth' to 'adult' femininity, is an irritation, or an anger even, which I have felt in witnessing what commonly seems to happen when rave and post-rave dance cultures come to be written about – within academia and pop journalism alike. To state the problem crudely (for the sake of introduction), girls and women just do *not* attract the attentions of youth cultural commentators. And this has been a relatively unchanging fact over the past decade. From the beginnings of my work, I found myself struggling within a cultural and academic climate in which statements like those made by Catherine, Jane and Teresa seemed to be prematurely dismissed as insignificant cultural signs, not worthy of the kind of status accorded the truth-claims of their male counterparts. At first, the accusations of empty populism, or over-excited celebration which I encountered in discussing my research interests did not particularly bother me. Admittedly it is problematic, but I was less interested at the time in engaging with debates about Cultural Studies' populism and more curious about what women were getting out of rave culture. I wanted to work first and foremost from this curiosity. But being told again and again, that what was *really* interesting about the advent of rave was how it had effected some kind of shift in *masculinity*, had slightly more effect on me, although I still had no idea at the time that such reaction would be something that I would spend so long wrestling with and writing about. Where at first I might have simply become annoyed, or just ignored or individualised such accusations, as my research developed, I very quickly came to recognise what I now view as an almost *regulated* denial of the place and practices of girls and women within club cultural criticism. From the dizzy heights of postmodern and poststructuralist theory, where the world looked like it was so rapidly changing, that all of our political agendas, language and interpretive frameworks had become long redundant, it was as if I had crashed back to a kind of 'old-fashioned' feminism – where all I could do was lament this denial, suffer the attendant frustration, and do little more than attempt to score-balance by putting girls back 'in the picture' so to speak. Alternatively, I could simply admit that there really *was* very little of interest to say about raving women, and accept that my own attachment to this area was as 'silly' as were these women's own attachments to night clubs. Angela McRobbie, in writing about the treatment of social dance by academics, touches upon the very familiar association between femininity, social dance and the 'unserious' which I have repeatedly encountered on many occasions, as she observes:

> And where dance has found its way into accounts of working class culture, it has tended to be either derided as trivial or else seen as a sign of moral degeneration. In his well-known study of Salford in the 1920s, *The Classic Slum*, Robert Roberts (Roberts, 1971: 222–5) combines both of these attitudes, linking the popularity of the mass dancehalls with the inherently unserious attitudes of young women. Richard Hoggart also thought that girls were 'silly' in this way (Hoggart, 1957: 50–1). In *Uses of Literacy* he accused them of having an almost unhealthy interest in all the paraphernalia of femininity and described them as 'surely ... flighty, careless and inane?' (1984, p. 132)

Clearly, resigning myself to the 'silliness' of my research interests was not an option. And anyway, this kind of discursive backdrop came to really fascinate me. Why and how, I wanted to know, did raving women make such fleeting appearances within the fast growing area of club cultural criticism? Part I of this work, entitled

Who Knows? (and I shall say more about the book's two parts shortly) is therefore dedicated to examining this question and to spelling out the steps which need to be taken in order that the stories of women like those quoted above can be considered culturally *significant;* meaningful 'signs' of our times. Here, I explore the numerous forces within club cultural criticism which appear to operate in prioritising what are predominantly male sites of experience and practice.

Part II of the book, *From Bedroom Culture to Dance Cultures* deals directly with analyses of my own data. This does not mean any strict division of criticism from analysis however, or that this book falls neatly into two parts. Although interview data are not thoroughly or properly discussed until Chapter 3, where relevant, interview extracts are brought into communication with academic criticism much earlier. These extracts should serve to write a background – to give an idea of the gap between the discourses of raving women and those of academic commentators. They frequently act as contestations to the dominant stories and histories coming to cohere around club cultures. But the point is clearly not about juxtaposing some 'reality' with academic 'interpretation' (and much more will be said about the status of the interviewee account in Chapter 2). It is simply about illustrating some very different – and very differently privileged – representations of rave and about indicating how some dominate, becoming the stuff of knowledge and history, whilst others simple do not *matter.*

Who knows? Mapping a backdrop of relative invisibility

Over the past decade, club cultures have become the subject of an animated and fast-growing discussion between youth and popular cultural scholars. As I have already suggested however, this debate tends to remain very firmly centred around various aspects of masculinity, whilst femininity and questions about the experiences of clubbing women, remain largely ignored.[3] This book is intended as an intervention into this discursive terrain. In particular, it sets out to challenge three common tendencies which can be seen to mark club cultural criticism and which all have the effect of 'writing girls out' or of simply not rendering them visible.

First, is the tendency to write about ravers in terms of sexless, ageless, raceless and otherwise non-specific or unsituated generals.

This tendency is often evident in works which take a *particular* 'post-modern' view of social dance cultures. Here, raving is seen to involve a sort of dissolution of the human subject. Identity, it is argued, disappears (Rietveld, 1993) and meaning evaporates (Mellechi, 1993) as ravers gradually lose their subjective belief in themselves, and merge into a bigger 'Body without Organs' (Jordan, 1995). Clearly, the sexually (or otherwise) specific subject has little place within such 'post-subject' scenarios. In Chapters 1 and 2, I critically interrogate such accounts, in stressing the need to keep club cultural discussion grounded in relation to the lived actualities of *specific* cultural subjects.

The second tendency I want to take issue with in this analysis is the *particular* 'feminist' inclination – characterised perhaps most clearly within Sarah Thornton's *Club Cultures: Music, Media and Subcultural Capital* (1995) – to state (and as I shall suggest, to unwittingly reinforce) the male-centredness of contemporary club cultures. Thornton's is an indisputably important, interesting and insightful work but unfortunately women and questions about femininity find little place within it. In paying such scant attention to the place, practices and experiences of women within these cultures (*because*, she argues, these cultures are not *about* femininity and if anything, they are structured in terms of a distance from signifiers of femininity) for me, Thornton actually colludes in reinforcing the very hierarchy she seeks to expose and criticise. She observes that in terms of dance event organisation and techno-musical production, club cultures tend to be male-dominated and such an observation is very clearly worth stressing. But I want to suggest that her failure to go *beyond* the levels of production and organisation, to say *more* about other levels of event participation and other experiential sites, amounts to a failure to address the significance of club cultural involvement for the hundreds of thousands of women who regularly participate in dance cultures, and who claim that such participation is central to their lives, their friendships and their identities. I want to argue therefore, that it is simply inadequate to focus so exclusively on the levels of dance musical production and event organisation if we want to explore issues of femininity. These levels *are* predominantly male sites of experience, but to prematurely conclude at this observation is insufficient. It does little to challenge what comes to be considered culturally significant about today's dance cultures: what actually gets attended to, written about and presented as knowledge. And although such a conclusion might be intended as a feminist critique of a particular form of male-domination, it does little to actually contest such domination. Knowledge is, as feminist epistemologists have long reminded us, *itself* an effect of domination.

A third tendency marking this field of debate is more common within pop and music journalism. Here, the approach to history-writing is (not surprisingly) even less critical than one tends to find within academic commentary. Club cultural history is stated as though this were simply an act of recording truth and reporting on reality. A list of primarily male innovators, organisers, musicians and producers thus becomes the skeleton around which *the* history of rave is fleshed out.[4]

Against this backdrop, it is not easy to call for the serious treatment of clubbing and raving women's own claims that their practices are somehow sexually 'liberating'. Taking such claims too seriously sounds either 'old-fashioned' (like hanging onto sexual specificity when we're in the exciting era of 'post-gender') or a little like denial (like naively celebrating something sexually 'positive' when *in reality* dance cultures are so heavily male-dominated). In defence of such a treatment I would first stress the political urgency of the need to hold onto the sexual specificity of the subject and second the fact that such a treatment need not involve a denial of any sexism or male-domination which might be seen to mark *one* level of contemporary dance cultures. Rather, and in a similar vein to Richard Dyer's treatment of 1970s Disco, I simply want to resist assuming in advance how a culture which might superficially appear sexist or otherwise discriminatory or oppressive, is used and made sense of by some of those who regularly participate within this (Dyer, 1990). In order to properly grasp the complexities of such understandings and usage, we need to attend more closely to how a particular cultural participation comes to mean to actual subjects and groups.

We need, I am arguing, a change of focus. An 'objectivist' history of contemporary club cultures – which might weave itself around the release of particular musical tracks, the set-up of particular record labels, the organisation of particular events or clubs, the media generation of particular moral panics or the various governmental attempts made at legislative intervention into Britain's 'party' scene – will reveal very little about how a large proportion of 'ordinary' clubbers and ravers have actually *used* and *experienced* club cultures over the past decade. It will show even less about *female* ravers and clubbers because women tend not to be located at the more visible – and the traditionally more 'meaningful' – levels of club cultures; the levels which attract most academic and pop journalistic attention. If women remain relatively invisible at these levels, then cultural commentators *can* make this invisibility twofold, by reinforcing a particular vision of what constitutes 'significant' cultural participation. A history concentrated around 'big' names, 'big' events, 'big' tracks, and so forth will afford femininity only a very brief and fleeting appearance. A focus upon the tabloid press's construction of rave's folk devils and its generation of particular moral panics, will likewise tend to make for a story which is primarily about young men; about 'fiendish' drug-dealers, 'dangerous' sexual predators, or uncontrollable football 'hooligans' (Redhead, 1994). Such foci – although they are the bases of many interesting (and often critical) club cultural commentaries – tend however, to strengthen a particular threshold of visibility through which only certain cultural movements, subjects and pracices are afforded passage. In order that *different* involvements within club cultures be rendered visible, we need to alter our focus. The present analysis does this. It shifts focus away from those sites which are traditionally seen to house significance, and concentrates instead upon the experiential accounts of a group of raving and clubbing women. If club cultures can be seen to signal or inscribe themselves in terms of vinyl, in architectural, technological or chemical terms, in terms of the event flier, the 12-inch 'white label' or the 'panic' press report, then *Club Cultures and Female Subjectivity* examines how they signal or inscribe themselves in terms of the lived experiences of particular women. If objects such as the above are allowed to tell a history of rave culture, then the present work attempts to use experience as different material to tell other stories. As Donna Haraway puts it 'experience is a semiosis. An embodying of meaning' (1991, p. 109).

Building and analysis around raving women's experiential accounts does however, clearly require some explanation and justification. Does this project not sound a little 'innocent' – a little over-simplistic and naïve in the credibility it seems to accord both the category of 'experience' and that of 'women'? Our poststructuralist scepticism about the experiential account, our reluctance to speak about the category of 'women' (because of the homogenising and appropriating effects that this can have), and our wariness of (evolutionary sounding) narratives of sexual-political 'progress', are all developments of which I am well aware. But we can work *with* such developments rather than allowing them to become yet another means by which certain cultural subjects are written out of history. The present is also, therefore, a work about the development of a poststructuralist or post-foundational approach to ethnography and the experiential account. Such a development is, as Angela McRobbie argues, desperately needed if we seriously plan to keep our research grounded in the lived (1997a).

Shifting femininities: from bedroom culture to dance cultures

Part I of *Club Cultures and Female Subjectivity* therefore deals with the relative invisibility of women within contemporary club cultural criticism. Of course, in one sense, there is nothing new or particularly surprising about this invisibility. Over fifteen years ago, McRobbie along with Mica Nava observed the extent to which Left interest in popular culture had made for an almost automatic association between the category of 'youth' and that of 'masculinity'. The terms, they explained, had become almost synonymous. In light of this, their own project was:

> To move away from a preoccupation with youth as deviant, youth as spectacular, youth as a peculiarly and unproblematically male genus. (1984, p. ix)

Unfortunately – and despite the fact that within the mass media at least, we have heard much about the advent of an apparent 'girl power' and about the birth of the so-called post-feminist 'ladette' – Left theorists seem to remain largely fixated upon cultural practices and sites of cultural experience which are still predominantly male. Making sense of the academic neglect of girls' cultural practices is not however, as easy as it might once have been. The male-centredness of club cultural studies can no longer be attributed to the fact that women simply do not participate in the more spectacular, 'adventurous' and attention-grabbing street-cultures which have traditionally interested youth-cultural scholars. So, whilst fifteen years ago McRobbie and Nava could quite plausibly attribute the failure to study girls to the fact that girls' cultural practices tended to take place largely within the domestic or familiar spheres (which simply do not attract as much attention as do the 'street', the 'deviant' or the 'ritual of resistance' for example), this argument no longer holds up. And whilst ten years ago, Rumsey and Little's (1989) argument – that the stories favoured by rock scholars had little to do with girls, because girls could not so easily partake of the kinds of 'unsupervised adventures' which these scholars celebrated – seemed valid, this is no longer the case. The cultural practices of girls and women are no longer so clearly confined to the home or to the bedroom. To argue therefore, that girls are ignored simply because they are somehow out of view, no longer makes sense. They *are* in view, but this presence is clearly still not enough to render them visible.

At the start of the new millennium, girls and women regularly rave, take drugs and stay out dancing all night. (Henderson, 1997; Pini, 1997a, 1997b, 1998, 2000). Even the home is no longer a 'safe retreat' from the 'street'; a comfortable haven wherein girls engage with the outside world of romance and rock culture through gazing at pop posters and losing themselves in the worlds of romantic fiction. The tragic death of Leah Betts demonstrated only too clearly how the 'home' (and in this case, one in which an ex-policeman and a nurse were guardians, and present at the time) can no longer be viewed as the safe and feminine 'other' to the dangers posed by 'the street'. This incident did something to deeply threaten not only our notions about the 'innocence' of adolescent girl-culture, but also about the safety from 'the street' supposedly guaranteed to women by domestic closure. And it brought to the fore the fact that girls are now more regularly partaking of practices which have traditionally been thought of as male.

Although it did not take this unfortunate death to inform us that social drug-use is no longer a predominantly male activity, it *did* drive home the naïvety of imagining that girls just aren't interested in cultural practices associated (however problematic such an association might be) with 'adventure' and 'danger'. We have come a long way then, from the situation described in 1978 by McRobbie who noted that:

So intransigently male are the mythologies and rituals attached to regular drug-taking that few women feel the slightest interest in their literary, cinematic or cultural expressions – from William Boroughs' catalogues of destructive self-abuse and Jack Kerouac's stream-of-consciousness drinking sprees to Paul Willis' lads and their alcoholic bravado. It would be foolish to imagine that women do not take drugs – isolated housewives are amongst the heaviest drug-users and girls in their late teens are one of the latest groups among attempted suicides by drug overdose. Instead, I am suggesting that for a complex of reasons the imaginary solutions which drugs may offer boys do not have the same attraction for girls. One reason is probably the commonsense wisdom deeply inscribed in most women's consciousness – that boys do not like girls who drink, take speed and so on; that losing control spells sexual danger; and that drinking and taking drugs harm physical appearance. (1978, reprinted in 1991, p. 29)

Female drug taking is no longer so heavily associated with personal pathology or with isolation. It has become acceptable and *social*. And as far as the perceived relations between drug-taking and female physical appearance go, these too have changed dramatically. If anything, a certain 'street credibility' now attaches to looking 'out of it'. My own interview data illustrate this very clearly, but so too did the appearance in the world of high fashion of so-called 'heroin chic'. Being 'out of it' is, for a number of reasons, no longer something which young women feel they need or want to avoid, for fear of losing control, endangering themselves or appearing sexually 'unattractive'. On the contrary, and as many of the present interviewees frequently point out, looking 'out of it' has come to be considered positively attractive:

If you've got a horny man that's smiling at you, it's like 'yeah'. When you're off your head, he likes it you know. I think a man *loves* a woman that's off her face – 'cause that's when you'll get a smile. (Jean)

Yeah, it gets much sexier when everyone looks off their face. Everyone just looks so much better and sexier and you know you do *too*. (Clare)

I love a man that looks off his face and the women too. Like women and everyone just look so much better when you're out of it. (Angie)

Contemporary figurations of femininity are not as tightly woven around notions about sobriety, dependency and closure as they once were. A 'new breed of women' announces the *Daily Telegraph* for example, can be spotted drinking in bars, clubs and pubs all around the country, consuming more alcohol than any previous generation of women. The 'ladette', because of her increased social and economic status, is turning to leisure sites and practices traditionally associated with men. 'Pubbing' and frequent bouts of excessive drinking have become normal practices for today's women. (19 April 2000) Being 'out of it' has simply become more attractive, possible and normal for girls and women. Whether this means being 'out of one's head', or simply being outdoors, alone and at night, some significant modifications to traditional fictions of femininity are being suggested. Such modifications speak through the various experiential accounts around which the present work is structured. As will become clear, sobriety, closure, caution and safety (all of which have traditionally been associated with femininity) figure very marginally within such accounts. Instead, these tend to be woven around episodes of often lone journeys during the night, into geographically unfamiliar places, within which mental 'trips' to similarly unknown places are made possible. The following claim is, for example, characteristic of these interviewees' experiential accounts:

> I would feel totally comfortable going to a rave solo, unlike discos and many pubs (people may look at you as being there to pick someone up). But I wouldn't hesitate to go raving on my own. It's fine for a woman to go to a rave, pop anything they want to, skin-up a huge joint and no one bats an eyelid. (Ann)

The story from which this extract is taken suggests the very different versions of femininity which are currently available to, and embodied by, many of today's young women. Like many of the other interviewees, Ann offers a story which is far closer to the 'adventure' narrative than it is to the 'homestead' fictions traditionally seen as characteristic of *girls'* stories. What raving appears to offer these women are the conditions of possibility for experiences of adventure, exploration and discovery: experiences which are often denied them within other spheres of their lives and which might also be viewed in the terms outlined by certain subcultural theory as constituting attempts to 'magically resolve' some of the contradictions and tensions which are coming to mark contemporary femininity. I shall return to this suggestion later.

If Ann's story is a narrative of 'adventure', then this is not simply about a *physical* adventure within a *physical* geography. It is also about a *mental* adventure and a *mental* geography. As Rosi Braidotti – whose work on Nomadic Subjects I shall return to later – argues:

> Not all nomads are world travellers; some of the greatest trips can take place without physically moving from one's habitat. It is the subversion of set conventions that defines the nomadic state, not the literal act of travelling. (1994, p. 5)

The present is a study of *both* kinds of movement, the argument being that movement into the world of raves and clubs often appears to allow for a kind of 'subversive' mental travel, or for what might be thought of as a disarticulation of traditional modes of femininity. It appears, that is, to allow for an imagining *beyond* these ways of being. Dick Hebdige, in discussing post-war subcultures, turns to John Berger as he reminds us that cultural landmarks are not only geographic but these are also biographical and personal (1987, p. 74). After the war, the traditional and familiar landmarks of social class had disappeared leaving a whole way of life in a state of collapse. Much the same might be thought of contemporary modes of femininity. With the erosion of recognisable signposts or landmarks, femininity is currently in a state of uncertainty and reconstruction. The 'elsewheres' or 'other worlds' opened up through raving are, I want to argue, particularly significant sites for expressing and exploring what can be thought of as a collapse of femininity's traditional landmarks. The fictions of femininity which we find emerging within raving women's accounts are, in terms of both literal and mental travel; in terms of both geographic and personal landmarks, radically challenging to the long tradition described by Carolyn Heilbrun, who observes that:

> Safety and closure, which have always been held out to women as the ideals of female destiny, are not places of adventure, or experience, or life. Safety and closure (and enclosure) . . . forbid life to be experienced directly. (1989, p. 20)

Of course and to reiterate, working as I am with women's experiential accounts, may not only seem naïve or like a simple celebration of femininity. It might also appear to be intended in a sort of 'hidden from history' vein. This is not the case, however. The present study is intended as much more than a simple score-balancing act. The point is not about exploring women's club cultural experiences, *simply* for the sake of it, or *simply* because we do not hear enough about such experiences. The motivation for the present comes from the fact that I believe that the stories raving women tell say a lot about available and emerging fictions of femininity. Contemporary club cultures are places where important questions about femininity are being asked, worked out and reworked; where alongside youth cultural 'statements' in general, important 'statements' are being made about new femininities. In part, what these statements seem to suggest is that femininity is currently undergoing an important dislocation from its conventional associations with the domestic and the 'natural'. Its traditional life-course and images of its 'rightful' place, are changing. As a landscape, femininity is being rearranged.

Although important differences exist within the group of women interviewed for this work, terms like 'freedom', 'liberation' and 'release' are central to all of their personal accounts of raving. What they claim to find within the rave event is entry into what Miriam calls a 'different world'; a 'world' within which they can be 'free', 'mad', 'out-of it' and 'off their faces' in ways which they simply cannot be in other spheres of their lives. Some are mothers. Some are students. Some are unemployed and some are in temporary jobs. Although all are white,[5] the women vary in terms of age and class background, and – although to a lesser extent – how they present themselves sexually. What unites them is the centrality which rave plays in their lives, and its importance in informing their understandings of themselves. Indeed, many claim to find both 'home' and their 'true' selves within the rave environment. Amy for example, says: 'When I discovered rave, I just finally found a place that felt like home – like being in the bosom of my family.'

If for these interviewees, raving can feel like being 'at home', then home is no longer a place of stability, familiarity or enclosure. Rather, it is a place which is temporary and fleeting. It is filled with 'madness' and 'confusion' and occupied by largely anonymous others. In it lie 'adventure' and the possibilities for experiences of self, which are new, exhilarating and sometimes frightening. And within it lie the opportunities for challenges to the confines of normative heterosexual femininity; the potential for the playing out of what are arguably more 'auto-erotic' and fluid pleasures and senses of self. Although many speak of finding their 'true' selves and their 'true' homes within the rave environment, neither the concept of 'home' nor that of 'self' is lodged in the language of stability, fixity or the 'natural'. Very new and different images of home and of self emerge from this material and these suggest – among other things – the extent to which traditional ideas about heterosexual femininity's 'life course' are being upset.

Barbara Bradby makes an interesting observation in relation to what we can think of as an upset of traditional fictions of femininity. She argues that we are now witnessing a general 'prolongation of youth' which has been partly effected by a decoupling of women and motherhood. This manifests itself within rave dancing, she argues, which, when compared to the 'grinding pelvises', 'snogging' and 'heavy petting' which went on in clubs of twenty years ago, indicates new public displays of non-reproductive sexualities (1993: 165). Bradby is right to point to the emergence of new and non-reproductive sexualities as these are suggested and played out within contemporary social dance cultures. But rather than viewing such an emergence as indicative of a general extension of *youth*, it is perhaps more correct to see this as evidencing the formation of new modes of *adult* femininity. If reproduction and domestic 'enclosure' have traditionally been seen as heterosexual femininity's 'rightful' place, then the accounts of those women who favour an identification with 'House' over one with 'home' indicate significant challenges to this condition, and provide some important insights into how such changes are actually being lived.

Researching women and rave: this critical journey

Finally, a few words on the structure of this book. The experiential accounts with which I am working here, are not treated in terms of a singular or uniform critical discussion. Instead, they constitute food for thought about several different questions and are thus approached in several different ways. This is partly because of the richness and complexity of this body of data as a whole. For me, it raises some often very different questions, concerning issues of 'freedom', self-regulation, female belonging, community and to-be-looked-at-ness, to state just a few. But the different tones and approaches characterising this work are also testament to my own journey through the past eight years. As Lawrence Grossberg very nicely puts it, the metaphor of travel is well suited to intellectual practice because it:

> ...allows us to see the complexity of intellectual alliances and disputes: sometimes people travel with you, or near you, or against you; sometimes they help you, or distract you, or interrupt you, or redirect you; sometimes we take a wrong turn, or a detour, or a dead-end; sometimes we are 'hijacked' (Hall) by another position and sometimes we are the 'hijackers'. (1988, p. 377)

As researchers, we can never entirely know in advance what our research will entail, or to what specific issues it will be directed. Indeed, this is part of the pleasure, the surprises which spring from the unknown. In studying the contemporary culture through which we move, as this, in turn, moves through and around us, we cannot fail to be surprised, to change direction, to occasionally get swept away, get stuck or get propelled in an unanticipated direction. My work has been precisely this kind of journey.

When I began the research, it was within a different historical context. Rave was a relatively new cultural scene and no one could have properly predicted its endurance or its complex development. I began then, as a feminist interested in youth cultures. As academic attentions came to be directed towards the rave scene, I began my work with women ravers. To reiterate, one of my primary aims at this point was to explore why so many women appeared to see rave as a 'liberating' – and even a sexually 'progressive' – culture. In short, I wanted to understand why to many, rave came to be such a significant practice and scene. I therefore concentrated within these interviews upon the role that rave played within these women's lives. This initial phase of interviews made several things clear. First, that the rave dance floor was seen to afford an incomparable sense of 'liberation'. Second, that as a practice, raving was seen to open the way into some kind of 'elsewhere' in which subjectivity was stated 'otherwise'. Third, that rave culture was seen as a sexually 'progressive' one. And fourth, that raving could come to play a fundamentally important part within a woman's life.

But the data also made something else extremely clear. Not surprisingly, I soon found that instead of simply gathering straightforward descriptions about involvements within contemporary dance music scenes, I was actually getting far more complex stories about being a woman within eighties' and nineties' Britain; about the contradictions, pleasures, anxieties and desires which can be part of this situation. In Chapter 3, I introduce all of the interviewees individually, in order to illustrate what rave culture means to these women, and highlight the different issues which came to be tied up in weaving together personal narratives of rave cultural involvement. But, and precisely because my 'data' made this journey with me, I also became interested in bringing raving women's accounts into communication with some of the work on feminist figurations which I encountered on one of my many detours. It struck me as interesting, significant and exciting that the fictions which emerged from my data seemed to resonate so forcefully with the fictional/'Utopian' worlds being explored by feminist philosophers such as Donna Haraway (1991) and Rosi Braidotti (1994). In Chapter 4, I therefore present a reading of these parallels and discuss the usefulness of certain new feminist work in opening up some of the theory cages which separate fiction, Utopia and imagination from fact and reality, and which limit what comes to pass as 'proper' knowledge.

Time was passing, the landscape was changing and I was still conducting interviews. Whilst the interview material continued to reinforce the links which I had been exploring between dance cultures and ideas about 'liberation' it also opened up new questions. One interview in particular (conducted with two 19-year-olds, Sally and Jean), directed me towards a previously unaddressed area. What the account indicated was that a certain degree of anxiety, hard work and self-management was involved in the production of the particular state of being which was sought within the rave event. In light of this interview, I went back to the others and reread them in terms of the operations which seemed to be conducted in the production of an 'ecstatic' state. In Chapter 5, I therefore present an argument which pays more attention to the self-regulation involved in the constitution of a 'peak' moment.

Despite shifts and modifications in focus, approach and interpretation, all of this work addresses one central issue: what is involved for women in the practices of raving? The book approaches this question by focusing upon a set of interrelated issues. How are female experiences of motherhood, sexuality, aging, belonging, transcendence and physicality articulated within the stories women tell about their rave practices? What happens when women can now occupy night time spaces which have traditionally been largely the preserve of men? What kind of 'freedom' are women talking about when they describe the 'liberating' potential of rave? And what does all of this tell us about shifting femininities more generally? Superficially only, is this *just* a study about British rave culture. In actual terms, the tales which these women tell when asked about their rave practices, involve so much more.

Notes

1 The methodological approach taken for this study and details about all of the interviewees are outlined in Part II.
2 See for example, the work of Janice Radway, 1984.
3 Exceptions to this, of which Angela McRobbie's is the clearest, will be returned to later on.
4 Look for example, to *Time Out*'s June 1997 Cover Story, which reports on a ten-year history of Acid House and rave culture.
5 In many ways therefore, this sample is racially distinct. Although this was never intended to be a study of white women, all of the women who volunteered for interview, were white. I realised that in order to make this a more racially mixed sample, I would have to target more specifically black clubs and events. I did not however do this. Instead, I tried to work with what I had, and to stick with this specificity. Clearly, a whole different line of questioning could have been pursued in relation to the interview material and issues of white femininity. This would however, have constituted a different study altogether.

Part I
Who Knows?

1
Invisible Women in Increasingly Visible Club Cultures

> A given epistemological framework specifies not only what 'knowledge' is and how to recognise it, but who are 'knowers' and by what means someone becomes one, and also the means by which competing knowledge-claims are adjudicated and some rejected in favour of another/others. The question of epistemology then, is crucial, precisely *fundamental* for feminism. (Stanley and Wise, 1983, p. 188)

> The true representation of power is not of a big man beating a smaller man or woman. Power is the ability to take one's place in whatever discourse is essential to action and the right to have one's part matter. (Heilbrun, 1989, p. 18)

As Liz Stanley and Sue Wise point out, 'knowledge' and 'knowers' are never neutral terms. Asking questions about precisely *who* is seen to possess knowledge and *who* is credited with the status of the knower are, they argue, fundamental to a feminist project. In this chapter, I want to illustrate how a seemingly *regulated* ignoring of questions about femininity and female club-cultural experience, appears to be in operation within the fast-growing discursive landscape of club cultural criticism. It is not simply the case that female ravers and clubbers do not tend to get written about by academics, but also that when their voices, or the voices appearing to speak in their 'defence' *are* heard, these are commonly dismissed as 'ungrounded' or 'Utopian'. The analysis presented in this chapter is then, intended as a challenge to an interpretative framework and an academic gaze which fail, on a number of counts, to allow female club-cultural presence and experience to *matter*.

Laying the background

In 1989, Stuart Cosgrove claimed that rave was 'the most popular youth cultural movement in post-war Britain'. Figures cited in *The Times* in 1993 for example, indicated that with respect to legal events alone, one million young British people were raving on a weekly basis. Two years earlier, researcher Russell Newcombe had claimed that 'it would be no exaggeration to say that raving is now one of the main reasons for living for a huge group of socially diverse people aged between 15 to 35 years' (1991, p. 1). Although at the start of a new millennium, the term 'rave' is somewhat outdated, techno-musical events which last all night and at which the use of 'class A' drugs is normal, are as popular as ever.

One might expect however – given academia's traditional neglect of social dance, and its derision of social dance cultures (Ward, 1993; Thomas, 1997; Novak, in Thomas 1993) – that despite its popularity, rave would have attracted very little attention. But this has not been the case. In fact, rave culture appears to have had some quite fundamental effects in altering the traditional relations between Left scholarship and social dance cultures. It is not my intention to fully describe such shifts although reference may be made to a piece by Dave Hesmondhalgh (1997) who critically surveys some of these. What I *do* want to do here, is demonstrate how despite the fact that an arguably unprecedented amount of academic interest is now being directed towards dance cultures, questions of femininity remain largely marginal to this fast-growing area of discussion. This is noteworthy however, *not* because it constitutes yet another instance of a prioritisation by scholars of cultural practices which are associated primarily with men and masculinity. On the contrary, this situation is particularly interesting precisely because social dance has long been thought of as a largely 'feminine' practice. Indeed, its well-documented neglect by scholars has tended to be attributed to what has variously been articulated as a neglect/fear/denial/derision of femininity, or of the 'masses' (which as Sarah Thornton demonstrates, is, as a concept, gendered feminine) more generally (McRobbie, 1991; Thomas, 1993; McClary, 1994).

We have come to believe then, that dance's neglect by academics is inextricably related to a more general neglect of femininity and of practices associated with this. Following this logic, and in light of the enormous academic interest which has now come to be directed towards social dance cultures, we might be forgiven for expecting that femininity would be a central focus of this interest – that because social dance is now such a hotly debated topic amongst cultural analysts, then so too is femininity. But, this is where the logic breaks down. The questions which we might expect to see addressed within something called 'dance cultural criticism' – questions about femininity, about the conditions and experiences of girls within nightclubs, or about the relations between raving, gender, desire and identity, are largely absent. Angela McRobbie's important account of club cultures and 'changing modes of femininity' (1994) and Sheila Henderson's (1997) work with young women clubbers (although this is less analytical than McRobbie's) are probably the only two works which deal with these issues in any great depth.

Contrary to claims that club cultural commentary has been dominated by questions about sexuality and gender (Hesmondhalgh, 1997; Thornton, 1995) I am arguing that in reality, women's club-cultural involvements have received very little attention. Their participation within, and understandings of these remain relatively absent as topics of research and seem therefore, to be relatively unimportant to those seeking to examine this area. This is the case from a number of significantly different perspectival stances which were touched upon in the introductory chapter and which will be returned to shortly. But first, it is worth briefly surveying some of the changes which have recently taken place in the relations between Left scholarship and social dance cultures.

The academic Left and new dance cultures

Critics have argued that dance cultures have traditionally been neglected by Left academia not only because of their associations with femininity, but also because of their associations with hedonism, 'unauthenticity', escapism and capitalism (Dyer, 1979; reprinted 1990; McRobbie, 1984; McClary, 1994). Early rave culture would seem to have done very little to challenge these associations. Its emphasis on physicality (as opposed to political consciousness) and its celebration of pleasure (as opposed to political struggle) could not have signalled a greater departure from certain Left models of youth 'resistance', or ignited more forcefully what Andrew Ross calls a 'paternalist concern over music's all-too-powerful sway over the minds and bodies of youth' (1994: 6). Not surprisingly, given the investments placed by Left academia in a particular notion of youth 'resistance', narratives of youth cultural history have tended to be 'punktuated' in such a way as to make 1970s punk the either implicit or explicit yardstick against which all subsequent youth cultures have been assessed. In so very many respects, early rave culture – as an ethos, a spectacle and a movement – could not have been further from punk. Rave's 'smiley face' logo, its 'shut-up-and-dance' ethos and its generation of a theme of ecstatic 'positivity' could not have been more seemingly opposed to punk's staging of youthful disillusionment. As Hesmondhalgh rightly notes, Punk represented 'an unprecedented overlap between the Left and popular culture' (1997: 170). Here was a movement which seemed to symbolise and ritualise dissatisfaction, aggressive retaliation and blank oppositionality, a movement which appeared to validate familiar Left investments in the potential of youth to 'resist'. It is no surprise therefore, to find that rave has more than once been unfavourably compared to punk (McRobbie, 1994; Hesmondhalgh, 1995). McRobbie, for example, stresses that 'rave contains nothing like the aggressive political character found in punk music' (1994: 168).

To many on the Left, early Acid House can have looked like little more than an uncritical embrace of 1980s' conservatism. It appears, as McRobbie suggests, to lack anything of the angry political character which made punk so interesting to youth scholars. In many respects, it bore all the markings of an unquestioning acceptance of individualist enterprise culture at its most extreme. The Acid House party at which young people took ecstasy and danced all night to techno-music, appeared to provide a perfect illustration of all that had been traditionally despised by certain Left cultural critics. The 'Trance-dance' for instance, could not have more clearly exemplified the kind of crowd *obedience* and *mindlessness* which Sarah Thornton writes about in commenting upon traditional Left response to dance musics and cultures:

Nothing could better signify the 'complete disappearance of a culture of meaning and aesthetic sensibility' says postmodern cultural commentator Jean Baudrillard, than a 'spinning of strobe lights and gyroscopes streaking the space whose moving pedestal is created by the crowd (Baudrillard, 1982: 5). Baudrillard's dismissal of the discotheque as the lowest form of contemporary entertainment reiterates a well-established view. Dance music has been considered to be standardised, mindless and banal, while dancers have been regarded as narcotised, conformist and easily manipulated. Even Theodore Adorno, an early theorist of mass culture, reserved some of his most damning prose for the 'rhythmic obedience' of jitterbug dancers, arguing that 'the music immediately expressed their desire to obey' and that its regular beat suggested 'coordinated battalions of mechanical collectivity . . . thus do the obedient inherit the earth. (Adorno, 1990: 312, quoted in Thornton, 1995, p. 1)

Susan McClary points to a similar degrading of dance musics, in talking about academic Left anxieties around the physical, the sensual and by extension, the feminine:

To be sure, Adorno is arguing in his vituperations against jazz for the continued preeminence of high art over popular culture. Yet those who purport to speak for popular culture have often reproduced this fear of the feminine, the body and the sensual. Recall for instance, the erasure of women – whether the blues queens of the 1920's or the girl groups of the early sixties – from historical narratives, or the continuing devaluation of dance music as a pathetic successor to the politically potent music of the sixties – especially in the 'DISCO SUCKS' campaign, where an underlying homophobia is quite obvious, but also in the blanket dismissals of the many African-American genres (including disco) that are designed to maximise physical pleasure. (1994, p. 32)

The hostility which characterised this kind of Left reaction to disco, was, as Richard Dyer argues, very clearly wrapped up in an understanding of dance music as capitalist, artificial and unauthentic. The yardstick against which disco was measured, Dyer argues, was a particular form of more apparently 'authentic' music, which involved both thematically and in terms of its production, a 'grass-roots' ideal. Compared to this romantic and naïve image of technologically unaided and independently produced songs about a bygone and 'simple' age, disco appeared artificial, materialistic and 'irredeemably capitalistic' (1979, p. 12).

Against a traditional academic Left backdrop which demanded that in order to be culturally 'significant', youth movements and musics had to conform to very particular notions about both 'resistance' and 'authenticity', 1980s Acid House looks as empty, conservative and de-politicising as did Disco in the 1970s. As a youth culture, it seemed to embody everything about dance-music that cultural critics as diverse as Adorno and Baudrillard have scorned the 'mindless', 'obedient' masses for. Aside from the appearance of absolute absorption and uniformity given by a 'trance-dancing' crowd, the heavy use of empathetic drugs and the heightened level of 'positivity' produced by these, made for a seemingly unashamed spectacle of youth hypnosis, narcotisation or anaesthetisation. Added to this, the financial cost of entering many dance events and buying drugs would seem to firmly seal rave's identity as a culture of conservative, capitalist consumption.

At its beginnings then, Acid House culture, and what soon became the rave scene, would seem to have done very little in challenging certain Left academic views of dance cultures as mind-numbing and de-politicising. But something has very obviously changed. The enormous interest which has now come to be directed towards dance cultures indicates a rather surprising turn-about in the reactions of Left scholarship. Clearly, rave's continuing and growing appeal to different youth groups, its complex development, plus its politicisation in the light of the introduction of the Criminal Justice Bill (CJB) have all made it more difficult to ignore as a highly significant cultural phenomenon. And this is evidenced by the ever-growing number of academic works being published, and conference papers being delivered, on various aspects of dance cultures. Equally relevant to this growing academic interest are technological developments which have made for important changes within the sphere of musical production – and which have thus made rave significant to debates currently developing around contemporary techno-culture. Finally, within Left academic thinking itself, we have witnessed a loosening up of the investments placed in concepts like 'resistance', and the promise of a more sophisticated view of the relations between cultural practice, subjectivity and 'politics'.

For what is clearly a complex of reasons, dance cultures and music have finally captured the academic Left imagination. They have been debated in relation to issues as wide-ranging as new forms of musical production (Straw, 1993; Hesmondhalgh, 1997); urban oppositional movements (Huq, 1996; Gilbert, 1996); the politics of Deleuze and Guattari (Jordan, 1995); youth's accumulation of sub-cultural capital (Thornton, 1995); the dawning of a postmodern techno-age (Ross, 1994); the death of the musical author (Goodwin, 1990) and the undoing of the coherent individual of liberal humanism (Rietveld, 1993; Tag, 1993; Hamment, 1995).

Despite how radical, heterogenous and seductive this language and debate might at first appear however, in many ways little has actually changed. Superficially, this criticism appears to promise so much that is new – new terminology, new challenges, and invitations to new kinds of 'political' action and interpretation. We are urged for instance, to shift our focus from 'sub-cultures' to 'neo-tribes' (Muggleton, 1995); from depth to 'surface' (Redhead, 1993); from 'old' versions of political action to a reconsideration of rave in terms of Deleuze and Guattari's ideas about 'desiring-machines' and 'Bodies without Organs' (Jordan, 1995). We are advised to rethink the investments that Left scholars have traditionally placed in youth's potential for 'resistance' (Thrift, 1996), and we are asked to re-examine precisely how and by whom such a term has been defined (Ross, 1994).

What we are rarely invited to do however, is to ask questions about the relations between social dance and the constitution of feminine subjectivity; about the place of dance within women's lives; about the significance of the social dance floor as a site for exploring the boundaries of 'appropriate' being; about the kinds of sexual-political discourses generated between clubbing women, or about what dance might mean for 'those who are the sites of this meaning' (Ward, 1997: 19). Instead, concern still remains quite heavily focused on questions about youth 'resistance' (although the language used to articulate 'opposition' may have changed somewhat) and focus still rests primarily upon male-dominated levels of club involvement – be this in terms of the accumulation of what Thornton calls 'subcultural capital', or in terms of musical production, technological innovations or dance music's *textual* politics, which as Barbara Bradby accurately observes have attracted far more interest than have questions about dance music's *sexual* politics (1993). Angela McRobbie's important piece on dance cultures and changing modes of femininity, is an exception and I shall return to it shortly (McRobbie, 1994).

The club cultural levels which appear to attract most critical attention, continue to be primarily male-centred. Women tend not to be located at the levels of musical production, event organisation, drug-distribution and hence profit-making. Neither are they the 'folk devils' constructed in various early press moral panics about rave culture. Although their exclusion from these traditionally more significant sites is clearly not total, were we to chart an objectivist history of rave culture, focusing upon its more outwardly visible signs, women would make a very fleeting appearance.

At this point, I should stress that I do not fail to see the importance of club cultural work on musical production, on press generations of moral panics about rave and ecstasy, on the implications of legislative intervention into Britain's party scene, on the growth of 'freedom to party' movements and so forth. I simply want to point out the extent to which such work *can* have the effect of continuing a very familiar preoccupation with youth as that 'peculiarly and unproblematically male genus' which McRobbie and Nava referred to back in the early 1980s. And there really is ample evidence that this situation continues well into this new millennium. As feminists, surely we should at least question the ways in which rave histories are allowed to be dominated by stories about men. To more fully understand the operations of this domination, it is necessary to return to the three tendencies introduced in the previous chapter.

(i) The twofold invisibility of raving women: some 'feminist' interventions

Clearly, there have been certain feminist interventions into the field of club cultural criticism. Very often however, although this might have the effect of highlighting the male domination of *club cultures*, it does little by way of challenging the male-domination of *club cultural criticism*. We can accept that women are marginalised at the more visible, and traditionally more 'meaningful' levels of today's club cultures, but feminist assertions of this marginalisation – assertions which go no further than simply reminding us of it – can actually have the effect of reinforcing female invisibility and of keeping 'club-talk' a discussion about men and masculinity. Even Angela McRobbie's

1994 piece on rave and changing modes of femininity (although I single it out as one of the few attempts at shifting focus away from boys and masculinity) highlights one of the limitations of simply restating and lamenting the (albeit important) fact that women are absent at the levels of rave production and organisation. McRobbie argues that:

> Indeed rave seems to overturn many of the expectations and assumptions we might now have about youth cultures, and for this reason, reminds us of the dangers of looking for linear developments and progression, in let us say, the sexual politics of youth. Girls appear for example, to be less involved in the cultural production of rave, from the fliers to the events, to the Djing than their male counterparts. We can in no way be certain therefore, that the broader changing climate of sexual politics is reflected in rave. (1994, p. 168)

Important and noteworthy as it is that women are largely excluded from the traditionally more 'meaningful' levels of dance cultures, surely their undeniably heavy presence at *other* levels of these cultures is equally worthy of attention and commentary.

As I suggested earlier, Sarah Thornton's *Club Cultures: Music, Media and Subcultural Capital*, although a very important intervention into club cultural criticism, is also, I believe, exemplary of the tendency to double raving women's invisibility. In remaining so heavily focused upon something which is primarily the preserve of men – subcultural capital – and by going no further than simply lamenting women's lack of this, for me, *Club Cultures* ends up being centrally a study about contemporary modes of youthful masculinity.

In drawing upon and adapting the work of Pierre Bordieau, Thornton's analysis centres around the hierarchies of subcultural capital which club cultures tend to generate. This generation depends upon the construction of a 'mainstream' which is gendered feminine, and against which the idea of an 'underground' is created. Remaining 'cool' means remaining 'underground', which in turn involves the constant reinvention of 'insider' credentials. These hierarchies function, she claims, to separate the 'in' from the 'out', the 'cool' from the 'naff', the 'hip' from the 'straight', and so on. Because being 'uncool' or 'unhip' appears to be associated with being 'feminine', girls have little symbolic place within contemporary dance cultures. Where they *do* belong, they either concede defeat, or they try to achieve the 'cred' afforded their male counterparts, by distancing themselves from the 'handbag' culture of 'Sharon and Tracy'. As Thornton explains this:

> After age, the social difference along which (subcultural capital) aligns most systematically is, in fact gender. Girls and women often opt out of the game of 'hipness', refusing to compete and conceding defeat. They are inclined to identify their favourite music as 'chartpop' rather than specialist genres, then defend their taste with expressions like 'it's crap but I like it'. In so doing, they acknowledge the subcultural hierarchy and accept their position within it. (1995, pp. 178–9)

Although Thornton clearly wants to present a feminist critique of club cultural organisation, in one sense her approach appears to reinforce the very subcultural hierarchy it sets out to criticise. Because it remains so heavily centred upon male clubber involvement, male-centred economies of subcultural capital, and primarily male sites of club cultural experience, *Club Cultures* falls short in really or seriously attempting to understand what *else* might be going on for women. Several important questions simply do not get addressed within this analysis. What negotiations of femininity are going on, for example, whilst boys and young men are negotiating their places within youth hierarchies? And what is the status accorded the accumulation of clubbing experiences by women who are neither the producers of club cultures, nor the dictators of what comes to constitute 'cool'? To put this another way, what *other* hierarchies and meaning structures might inform how women read their club involvement? Where being 'cool' or 'hip' is less important than is just being out for 'a night with the girls' for instance, or where the significance of clubbing has far more to do with escaping the confines of a heterosexual partnership than it has with being 'in the know', what is going on? If Thornton's work concentrates upon a relentless drive to remain 'cool', then what other drives might fuel club cultural participation? Surely, and contrary to the image presented in *Club Cultures*, when it comes to talking about women, there must be *more* to note about femininity than its relative marginality at the level of event organisation and techno-musical production, and *more* to comment on than women's subordinate positions within the sub-cultural hierarchies which club cultures tend to generate.

This particular kind of 'feminist' critique of contemporary dance cultures (and Thornton is not alone in advancing it) enables us to say very little about actual women and *their* sites of clubbing experience, or *their* understandings of today's club cultures; little, that is, about anything other than their inferiority, marginality or subordination. Can – as Thornton seems to suggest – girls and women *really* be little more than compliant and defeatist subordinates within a boys' world where the 'cool' so endlessly chased by clubbers is achieved through a process of distancing from signifiers of femininity; where to be 'cool' is to be everything that femininity is *not*? Surely, girls themselves sometimes work to generate *different* hierarchies or economies of subcultural capital, different images of 'cool' and 'hip', and different notions of club cultural belonging.

Femininity, as it appears within this analysis, only ever exists in relation to one overarching hierarchical structure and women only ever have one of two kinds of relations to this structure. They can concede defeat, or they can differentiate themselves from 'Sharon and Tracy'. Such a reading is clearly limited inasmuch as it fails to explore any alternative subject positions and meanings structures, which might be open to raving and clubbing women. What is missing is an examination of how, for instance, a mainstream/subculture distinction might signify differently for men and women. My own research suggests for example, that such a distinction very often functions for women not simply to reinforce particular notions of 'cool' (other people's 'cool', or their own lack or possession of it) but it can also be called upon to reference important issues around sexual safety. Hence, the significance of distinguishing between 'mainstream' clubs (which are defined as those where 'pop' rather than 'techno' is played, where alcohol rather than drugs such as ecstasy is taken, and where sexual 'pick-up' rather than dance seems to be a primary motivation) and rave or post-rave events, is frequently tied up with some very basic practicalities about getting to and from an event, and with remaining 'safe' within an event. Here the 'mainstream' is evoked to signal what is frequently perceived to be an annoying or even threatening form of 'predatory' male behaviour. It is thus called upon in articulating a dissatisfaction or discomfort with traditional sexual relations and with the conventional limitations placed upon women's 'freedoms'. Here, the 'mainstream' is not so much about that which is 'naff', as it is about that which is seen to be sexually oppressive. And 'belonging' within a rave is not so much about being 'cool' as it is about being 'freed' from nightclub environments which feel like 'cattle-markets' (a term used by at least three of the present interviewees).

For many of the present interviewees, rave's major appeal lies in its provision of the opportunities for taking drugs, going 'mental' and dancing through the night without sexual harassment. If their involvement within rave is linked with being 'cool', then this is often a very different notion of 'cool' from that which operates for their male counterparts. The 'un-cool' is not so much the 'Sharon and Tracy' who dance around their handbags, as it is a general condition wherein girls and young women are denied access to unsupervised, night-time adventures. 'Cool' here, is not about the 'in' clubs, DJs, and records, it is about contesting the limits of traditionally 'appropriate' femininity. Indeed, in this respect, there is often a clear 'feminist' edge, or what McRobbie calls a 'semi-structure of feminist feeling' (1997b) evident within raving women's accounts of their contemporary club cultural involvement. Many of these women talk, for example, of clubs and raves being 'cool' because they can go to these alone and because unaccompanied women are not viewed as unusual, or as sexual 'prey'. Narratives of a sexual-political 'progress' thus frequently underpin their definitions of 'cool' clubs to a far greater degree than do narratives structured around subcultural capital accumulation. The following claims for instance, are characteristic of how many of these interviewees make sense of the advent of rave culture:

> The minute rave happened, it was all right for you to go out by yourself and you weren't going to get all that hassle. It's probably because men were there to dance, not pull or something. I didn't really like clubs before. Now raving is really important to me. As a woman you know that you're all right or much more safe than you would have been in an old-style dance-club where blokes are trying to harass you. (Clare)
>
> I remember my mum saying 'oh, you're really lucky 'cause I used to love dancing, but you couldn't do it without a partner'. And

I thought, yeah, that's really good. You can dance on your own. You don't need a man to ask you to dance or you don't need anyone to dance with. You don't even need anyone to go to a rave with. It's changing... If I went to clubs before I'd expect to get constant hassle and lots of kind of unwanted advances and quite pushy sort of ones as well. Now I go out on my own. If no one wants to come out, I *do* go alone. (Amy)

Before I started raving, I hated that pick-up aspect of clubs. There was always a feeling that you could fail – if you didn't get picked up and also, if you didn't get picked up by the right person then what was the point? There was always the idea – when you got approached – of God, are they going to demand something of me that I'm not going to give? Meaning a snog, or a fuck, or a date, or a phone number or whatever... Yeah, before rave it was the worst thing possible. There were lots of pissed men and a really lairy, letchy kind of space where you couldn't do anything without being interfered with. There were loads of pissed blokes and kind of out for the fucking lay. (Jane)

Before, I wouldn't feel safe going somewhere like that [a club] on my own, because I'd feel intimidated – probably for no reason, but I *would* feel intimidated and I wouldn't feel that I would have people respect my space. Now everyone knows that you've got this certain amount of space around you and no one seems to impinge upon that space. (Teresa)

The distinctions which the above women make between raves and pre-rave events are clearly far more heavily tied into differences between 'hassle' clubs and 'non-hassle' clubs, than they are about demonstrating some kind of 'in the know'. Indeed, in discussing their favourite and least favourite dance events, many of the present interviewees explicitly contradict (rather than bow to) the particular notions of 'cool' which Thornton discusses. 'Hard' machismo, for example, is frequently viewed as a transparently obvious and quite ridiculous attempt at remaining 'cool'. 'Giving it attitude', being 'moody', not 'letting off' or not 'letting go' (all of which are associated with a particularly excessive mode of 'street' masculinity as this is seen to be embodied by 'attitudies' or by the club 'bouncer' for example) are terms frequently called upon in criticising certain forms of male behaviour within raves and clubs. It is, then, often the signifiers of 'hard' *masculinity* rather than those of 'naff' femininity which are ridiculed and distanced from:

> At that particular one, they [the bouncers] were completely ridiculous. I mean well, you're hardly going to say anything 'cause they're built like ... Well, they're huge but I'm not joking, it's their chance to play Rambo and you know if they were on their own, they would *not* be so mouthy and you just see them giving it all the mouth, and those puffa jackets make their shoulders look even bigger and they're all on mobiles. It's their chance to play 'big boys' isn't it? (Clare)

> Some of them though [men in raves] just try and look so fucking cool, it's stupid. That guy at that [rave] on her birthday that we met, he was a right plonker. Really into it, wasn't he? Like Mr Big, thinking he was. We had no time for that did we? He was like one of those ravers who's like 'oh yeah, girlie, stupid'. (Chris)

> We're not like that you know. We're not those 'attitudies', giving it attitude like the blokes. We're happy ravers, aren't we? (Jean referring to herself and Sally)

Such reactions are very common, clearly suggesting that male-dominated notions of 'hard' and 'cool' do not pass unchallenged. Along with the many articulations of a particular 'we don't need men' discourse which emerges from these data (and to which I shall return), these reactions suggest the partiality of Thornton's picture. These factors speak of a different kind of clubber 'insider-ness' – one which has far less to do with respecting certain forms of 'cool' masculinity and far more to do with a kind of popular 'feminist' critique which appears to operate *within* club cultures themselves.

Although I have suggested that Thornton fails to acknowledge some of the complexities of female involvement within rave culture, this is not entirely straightforward. It is not simply that she fails to recognise *claims* for different kinds of female involvement in rave – claims that something about this culture might be sexually 'progressive'. Thornton *does* in fact engage with *claims* that perhaps women get something more from raving than what their humble position in male-dominated hierarchies afford them. But she reads such claims as *mistaken*, arguing that:

> In fact, so powerful are the feelings of 'liberation' afforded by the dance club that the most common argument about contemporary social dancing is that it empowers girls and women. However, these studies tend to conflate the *feeling* of freedom fostered by the discotheque environment with substantive political rights and freedoms. (1995, p. 21)

If women *do* find a place within Thornton's analysis, they thus appear to signal a kind of 'false consciousness'. Such women are little more than duped, overexcited or 'carried away'. Their claims are 'Utopian' and they fail to acknowledge the distinction made by Thornton between *feelings* of freedom and 'substantive political rights and freedoms'. They fail that is, to see things as they *really* are.

It is not entirely clear what Thornton means by 'substantive political rights and freedoms'. Neither is it clear precisely *who* she is referring to in speaking of these 'common arguments' – and I shall come back to this shortly. But even if we are simply talking about women's 'freedom' to party alone and unharassed, about their struggles to defend this 'freedom', or about their temporary release from the domestic and familial realms, then something crucial about the regulation of femininity is, I believe, at stake here. This *is* about politics. Consider, for instance the following claims:

> We're [referring to herself and Sally] single parents and we have to save 'cause we do our pills. You've got to save for them, and your ticket. I mean it's really expensive. I've got to think about Mick [her son] and get someone to look after him. My mum has him for a couple of days so when I get him back, my come-down's gone... But it's my time for me isn't it? He [her ex-boyfriend] tried to stop me going. But when he went to prison that was it. I got my life back. 'Cause he was well ... So I got my life back and got back into it [raving] basically. I can't see myself stopping for years. (Jean)

> He [her boyfriend] doesn't like me going out clubbing, but I'm not going to stop ... I don't think I can have clubbing *and* him for

much longer. I mean how long can I really go on like this and
expect him to stick around? It does piss me off, that I probably
will have to change. Mind you, I've said that before and part of
me is adamant to do what I want. It's my time for freedom. He has
his, and I want mine. (Clare)

For Jean and Clare, raving is very clearly tied into an issue about
their 'rights'. In both cases, the 'right' to rave is something which is
struggled for and it is something which has to be defended. Both, for
example, speak at length about various ongoing arguments with
their boyfriends about their 'freedom' to party – thus suggesting
some of the difficulties involved in juggling what are often seen to
be the seemingly incompatible positions of 'raver' and 'girlfriend',
or to put this another way, the tensions involved in struggling
between different and changing definitions of 'appropriate' heterosexual femininity.

But 'freedom' as it appears within these interviewees' accounts, is
not simply about negotiations with parents and lovers concerning
the 'rights' to go out at night to clubs and raves, or about the 'rights'
to dance unharassed by men once inside these. If these women speak
about the rave as offering a kind of release from the seemingly 'regulatory' gaze of boyfriends (and some describe deliberately 'losing' their
boyfriends within an event), from the responsibilities of motherhood, or from the advances of 'predatory' men, then there is also
a common thread running through these accounts concerning a
general loosening up of the rational or 'together' self within a rave
event. In particular, the frequent claim that rave affords them a
space for publicly 'going mad' or 'losing it' in a way which they
simply cannot within other spheres of their lives, suggests, I believe,
that the rave event is now a highly significant site for explorations
of the boundaries surrounding conventional modes of femininity.
Teresa for example, claims that the rave is so important to her,
because here she can go 'mad' and 'lose it' in a way that she simply
cannot within other areas of her life. For Sally and Jean, 'losing it' in
the rave environment allows them to be very different kinds of
women from who they are as mothers. Indeed, both are at pains to
keep these very different senses of self entirely separate. They thus
make sure that child-care provisions are in place not only whilst they
are raving, but also whilst they are 'coming down'. They simply

would not, they stress, be around their children during these times and this is not just because they feel that they might not be able to cope with child-care during 'come-down', but more because they do not want their children to see them in a state which is obviously more *self*-centred than usual:

> *Jean*: My mum has him for a couple of days so when I get him back, my come-down's gone.
>
> *Sally*: Yeah, when I go raving it's always on a Saturday night and I don't get her [daughter] back until the Monday. She goes to her dad's. Nah, you know what the weekend is and I mean, Sunday's out.
>
> *Jean*: Yeah, you got to make sure that the kids ain't around on the Saturday night or the Sunday. I wouldn't let him see me like if we're 'speeding' before we leave. Not speeding *or* come-down. I don't want him seeing me like that. I'm very different from normal and it would be weird for him.

Jane raises a similar point about how different from 'normal' she feels she can be within the rave event. The rave environment appears to afford her a very different sense of self from that which she embodies in her everyday life as a part-time counsellor:

> If say, one of my clients saw me when I was clubbing, or some-body who was from a professional day-world came and saw me clubbing, it would *not* be ideal. It's like oh no, I *don't* want that to happen. [Raving] is about letting go of being conformist, and being professional and proper and together. It's other to presenting that face of you. It's not necessarily the dark side of you. But it's the messy side of you. It's about doing whatever the fuck you want and without thinking you've got to be there for somebody else. It's being there for yourself and being 'off your face' and not having to really think about anybody else. (Jane)

An association between raving and 'madness' is common through-out this sample and indicates the extent to which the rave space is experienced by many of these women as one of release or freedom from the constraints surrounding them within their normal, every-day lives. For all of these women, the rave event provides a very important space for being something different and often this is about being able to 'lose it':

> Rave is about going to the edge, which represents the edge between sanity and insanity. It's about losing it. (Elaine)

> It's best for me when I feel like I can go completely mad – usually when I dance until I feel like I've expressed every single anxiety or pressure and it all comes out. It's like a safe space for going mad. (Amy)

> That first time was completely mad. I'd never known that kind of ... like feeling that free and carefree. Like I wasn't worrying about anything at all. It really did change me. I felt like I'd never let go before that. (Catherine)

It could of course, be argued that such sensations and the general 'loosening up' of rationality which raving can involve are not particular to women. Indeed, Jeremy Gilbert (1999) has argued that men too can experience, within the rave event, this sense of liberation from the strictures of gender. He is obviously correct. What is significant for the present study however, is the fact that a space for the public playing out of 'madness', for the open enjoyment of 'adventure' and for a communal exploration of self-focused pleasures, has traditionally been largely denied to women. Even today, very few cultural spaces exist within which women can safely and publicly perform 'madness'. Where boys and men have long been afforded the opportunities for 'unsupervised' night-time adventures; for getting 'off their faces'; for enjoying the kinds of transcendent experiences associated with drug-taking, and for being 'irresponsible' without the attendant pathologisation which has historically tended to mark the 'out-of-it' female as hysterical, endangered or sexually 'loose', girls and women have come to learn that their rightful place is the domestic, and that their rightful state is 'sanity' and responsibility. Within contemporary social dance scenes such ideas appear to be being subverted.

The argument that rave might be somehow 'empowering' for girls and women, is one which Thornton is eager to dismiss. Not only does such a dismissal appear to ignore the range of issues raised by the women quoted above, but it actually casts such women as 'mistaken'. Although Thornton is not really talking about ravers' *own* claims, but about those made by academic commentators (although this, too, is a little problematic and I shall return to it shortly), indirectly she constructs women like those quoted above, as being somehow *wrong* in their interpretations. They, like those academics who might speak 'positively' in their 'defence', are wrong, because their understandings are based upon a mistaken conflation between *feelings* of liberation and *real* rights and freedoms. But there is something even more problematic about this kind of dismissal of claims for any 'positive' sexual-political aspect to contemporary dance cultures (and Thornton is not alone in forwarding such a dismissal). This concerns the significantly shaky foundations upon which such dismissal is commonly based. Few, if any, critics actually ground such claims empirically. Even where *secondary* research is involved, there are problems. Dave Hesmondhalgh for example, claims that: 'Gender and sexual politics are areas where overexcited and unsupported claims for the radicalism of dance music are commonly heard' (1995, p. 9). And Barbara Bradby writes of the: 'Utopianism that has surrounded dance culture, which has a post-feminist side to it in its claims to have moved beyond sexism' (1993, p. 156).

In Hesmondhalgh's piece, no indication is given as to where precisely such claims are supposed to emanate from. Who exactly, we are left wondering, is making these overexcited and unsupported claims? Bradby too, offers little indication of where this 'Utopianism' is supposed to come from, although at one point in her piece, she does refer to an interview published in *New Musical Express*, in which a black rapper and his white partner speak of what she calls the 'egalitarian collectivism' of the rave scene. Thornton, who arguably launches the most severe attack on these apparently 'Utopian' claims, actually references Bradby: 'As Barbara Bradby argues, this kind of Utopianism ignores the subordinate position that women occupy at most levels of rave culture' (1996, p. 21).

Where Thornton attempts to more concretely ground the kinds of claims about rave which she wants to challenge, more problems emerge. To return to a statement cited previously, here Thornton is referring specifically to *contemporary* rave and club cultures:

In fact, so powerful are the feelings of 'liberation' afforded by the dance club that the most common argument about contemporary

> social dancing is that it empowers girls and women (c/f. Blum, 1966; Rust, 1969; McRobbie, 1994; Gotfrit, 1988). However, these studies tend to conflate the *feeling* of freedom fostered by the discotheque environment with substantive political rights and freedoms. (1995, p. 21)

Thornton offers as support for this claim about *contemporary* dance cultures, references from as far back as 1966. Angela McRobbie's 1994 piece *Dance and Fantasies of Achievement* is for example, very clearly dealing with pre-rave dance scenes such as the local discotheque and women's involvements within this. Hence, despite her claims to be addressing a *contemporary* context, Thornton makes no distinction between today's club cultures and those of over thirty years ago. To be fair to her work however, perhaps it is precisely because she aims to demolish such historical and cultural distinctions between dance cultural scenes, that Thornton refuses to draw a line between pre and post-rave events.

Accusations of Utopianism in relation to claims about the sexual politics of today's dance cultures are then, rather suspect. Contrary to what such accusations might suggest (and as I have repeatedly argued), the most visible commentaries on rave and post-rave dance cultures can be seen to be suggesting something quite different – either that rave is 'retrogressive' in terms of its sexual politics, 'empty' in terms of its meaning, or that it involves an 'undoing' of the (significantly ungendered) self. Recall for example, McRobbie's argument that 'we can in no way be certain therefore, that the broader changing climate of sexual politics is reflected in rave' (1994, p. 168) The actual picture being presented is then, far from 'over-excited', or even particularly optimistic. Rave is about 'avoidance' (McRobbie, 1994); about 'disappearance' (Rietveld, 1993); about 'loss' of identity (Mellechi, 1993) and so forth. McRobbie writes for example:

> There are so many dangers (drugs, cigarettes, alcohol, unprotected sex, sexual violence and rape, ecological disaster), so many social and political issues which have a direct bearing on their lives and so many demands made of them (to be fully responsible in their sexual activity, to become good citizens, to find a job and earn a living, to find a partner and have a family in a world where

marriage becomes a 'temporary contract') that rave turns away from this heavy load headlong into a culture of avoidance and almost pure abandon. (1994, p. 172)

In light of this, it appears that such accusations of Utopianism are themselves unsupported, or at very least a rather excessive reaction to what are clearly underinvestigated claims. And such reaction is telling. It appears to say much more about the concerns of certain critics than it does about what is actually going on within, or actually being said about, contemporary club cultures. Why, I want to ask, should this apparent Utopianism be of so much more interest to commentators, than the arguably far more significant fact that women are largely denied a voice or presence within dominant stories of rave? Why has so little empirical research gone into examining such claims? And why is there such an eagerness to dismiss claims which clearly have not even been fully articulated?

Even if we accept that a certain Utopianism might undermine claims for rave's sexually 'liberatory' potential, this is hardly a major problem. Neither is it particularly surprising. As Donna Haraway's work (1991) stresses, the visionary or the imaginary are never quite as distinct from the 'factual' as we might like to believe. We only need look to the development of British youth cultural studies for example, to see that Utopianism, imagination and romance have never been far from centre-stage. Do traditional investments in concepts like 'resistance' not speak a certain Utopianism? The whole notion of a resistant youth for instance, clearly betrays a quite romantic preoccupation on the part of Left scholarship with particular 'heroic' acts carried out by (usually male) youth. Few interpretative stances or situated knowledges, lack 'imagination' – a desire for something which does not yet exist. And just like more official or established stances, popular cultural knowledges can also be visionary. One of the values of Haraway's work (and also of that of Rosi Braidotti, to whom I shall return) is that it reminds us that in fact, the most illusory knowledge of all is that which fails to admit to the partiality and situation of its own make-up. Utopias as literally 'no places' are where the 'detached' and masterful scientist wants to reside as he plays 'god'. On the other hand, claims that in certain situations, rave appears to open up new possibilities, especially if such claims find plenty of empirical back-up (not as evidence of truth, but rather as evidence of a particular culturally meaningful and effective fiction), are quite legitimate and hardly, it would seem, deserving of the kind of dismissive reactions outlined above – particularly when such dismissal is directed towards a generally unspecified source. And it is particularly worrying perhaps, that those claims least likely to be considered grounded, or 'realistic' are those referring to the issue of sexual politics. Hence, those most likely to be 'mistaken' in their readings of club cultures are women like the following:

> For me there's nothing better. I feel completely safe and of course, you may get men giving you the eye but it really *is* entirely different to the club scenes I was involved in before. Something very important happened with rave and things have never gone back to what they were. It's the way that men and women behave towards each other. Mainly, like I said, I think it's because if you're in a dance event these days, you're there to *dance*. You're there to dance and not to pull. Everyone understands this and this is the greatest thing about it. Of course, you might *want* to pull and it's not out of the question, but something big is different. (Clare)

> (Rave) was strikingly different to other club scenes. There was no alcohol around, so little aggression and little emphasis on chatting people up, and the cattle-market element of say disco didn't seem to be around. (Ann)

> Rave is a completely different scene. Men seem very unaggressive. They're friendly in a completely different way from people being friendly when they're completely pissed-up. The men – even in the kind of hard-core clubs – aren't sort of predatory, and they're not there to pull. (Amy)

To return to the twofold invisibility of women mentioned earlier, a third level can now be added:

(i)   Women's experiences in the main, are not located at the more visible and traditionally more 'significant' levels of club cultures. These are predominantly male sites of experience;

(ii) Once reconstructed within pop and academic histories, rave is retold mainly in terms of these sites of experience. Male experience tends then, to be reconstructed as the significant object of history;

(iii) Any claims suggesting that women may actually get something positive out of their involvement within this male-dominated structure, are frequently dismissed as unsupported.

To reiterate, I consider *Club Cultures* to be a very important and informative account of *certain* aspects of today's dance scenes. But, it fails in adequately or seriously addressing precisely why women might come to associate clubbing with 'freedom' and 'liberation'. For Thornton, the answer lies not simply in some mistaken association between 'feelings' and 'real' politics, but it can also be found in looking to club architecture and design which work to produce what she calls 'other-worldly environments':

> Clubs however, offer other-worldly environments in which to escape; they act as interior havens with such presence that the dancers forget local time and place and sometimes even participate in an imaginary global village of dance sounds. Clubs achieve these effects with loud music, distracting interior design and lighting effects. British clubs rarely have windows through which to look into or out of the club. Classically, they have long winding corridors punctuated by a series of thresholds which separate inside from outside, private from public, the dictates of dance abandon from the routine of school, work and parental home. (1995: 21)

Of course, there is nothing wrong with this picture of the club environment. The problem however, is in viewing the 'other worlds' created within the club context as having no political or cultural significance or effectivity beyond their function as markers of an 'underground'. Even though such 'worlds' may well be as much the product of 'imagination' as they are of material, this does not undermine their significance as meaningful sites for the development of alternative stories of being, and hence, for the alternative identities which can arise through connection to such stories.

(ii) Disappearance, loss and post-identity

If concentrating, as Thornton does, upon the 'cool' veneer of club cultures and the people who represent this, tells us very little about the location and experiences of clubbing women, then one particular 'postmodern' approach to these cultures leaves questions about femininity equally untouched. But it does so in a different way. Here, it is not of particular concern that women within rave might occupy subordinate structural positions. Instead, these readings commonly present the raver as a non-sexed, non-raced, and otherwise non-specific generality. It is then, common to read about the 'undoing of the constructed self within rave' (Rietveld, 1993) or 'the definitively postmodern experience of the self' which characterises raving (Mellechi, 1993). Although much is made within such accounts of the so-called 'constructed self' which is apparently 'undone' in rave, little is said about precisely what *kind* of 'constructed' subjects we are talking about. This tendency to leave the raver unsexed and otherwise unmarked, is particularly apparent within the different works collected in Steve Redhead's *Rave Off* (1993). Here, the authors draw upon the work of Baudrillard in interpreting rave as a form of mass 'disappearance' which constitutes a postmodern collapse of meaning. This surrender to meaninglessness, argue various of the contributors, makes for a more radical form of challenge to Left scholarship because it resists appropriation into the arms of theory, and therefore obstructs the academic will to knowledge.

The sexed subject clearly finds little place within the kind of 'post-subject' scenarios which are presented within *Rave Off*. If rave signals a 'death' of meaning, and a 'death' of depth, then it is also very clearly seen to signal a 'death' of the sexed subject. Indeed, Antonio Mellechi explicitly states that attempting to hold onto identity classifications when it comes to talking about rave 'completely misses the point'.

> Those who sought to understand this subculture in terms of a politics and usage and identity completely missed the point. The spaces which club culture occupied and transformed through Ecstasy and travel (retreating into the body, holidaying in Ibiza and Rimini) represent a fantasy of liberation, an escape from identity (1993, p. 37)

Although it is true that ravers may well experience a sense of 'losing' themselves within an event, this does not mean that identity has been 'escaped' from. Body-subjects within rave may well experience

a sense of merging into a larger 'body' (such as the 'body' of the dancing crowd) but as far as raving women go, this does not mean that
femininity is ever fully 'escaped' from. Or to put this in Barbara Bradby's
language, ravers may well articulate different ways of construing the
body and the world within an event but this does not amount to a loss
of 'identity'. All of the present interviewees for example, when asked
about the experience of raving, speak at once about sensations of
'loss' *and* an ongoing awareness of their sex and their sexual safety.
The sensations of which they repeatedly speak are intensely *physical*
and they are about an acute awareness of their bodies, their cultural
markings, and their interrelations with other bodies – rather than
about any kind of disappearance from embodied identity.

Something else is lacking from such 'loss of identity' arguments.
This is a recognition that rather than enabling people to 'lose' their
identities, raving is very often about the *consolidation* of an identity.
It is very clear for example, that in identifying themselves as 'ravers'
many of the women I interviewed, were staking claims on a view of
themselves as women of a *particular* kind. Sometimes this meant
claiming an identity as 'non-conformist' or 'non-traditional'. The
identification becomes a kind of shorthand for a whole host of statements about being dissatisfied with conventional sexual-relations,
being unwilling to 'settle down', being a 'mad' or 'wild' woman,
being *not* like 'good girls' who never take drugs, never go to all-night
events, and who would never go dancing alone. Catherine says for
example:

> They [her friends] just weren't into that kind of thing [raving].
> We'd all been into gigs and pubs and that's all. I lost them all
> 'cause they were all cosy-cosy by the time I got into raving and
> still just wanted to pub it and be nice and safe in [her hometown]
> and it all ended. They're the kind of women – I suppose they're
> still the same – who would never touch a pill or . . . they would
> think it was mad. I think they've probably all settled down at
> home now. I hear about some of them from my mate here in
> London, and it makes me so pleased and just happy I'm not like
> that any more.

The argument that to read rave in terms of identity constitutes
a complete missing of the point, obviously fails to take account of

the fact that for some people, staking out an identity as a raver is a highly significant move.

Mellechi's argument is also problematic because in many respects, it very much contradicts his *own* reliance upon particular 'identities' in making his points. He seems, that is, to have little difficulty with asserting the important role played by certain (almost exclusively male) musicians and DJs in the development of this culture. These 'identities', it seems, remain very much alive. Interestingly, in writing about contemporary musical production, Barbara Bradby notes that recent discussion of techno-music has been almost entirely dominated by two centrally male concerns: the 'death' of the author, and the 'death' of history. The same is true of much discussion of dance cultures generally. Interestingly, arguments such as those presented within *Rave Off* indicate how contradictory are such concerns. History is written. Names are named. Yet we are simultaneously reminded that this is not about linearity or identity. It is about death and disappearance.

Against this kind of 'postmodern' backdrop, keeping a grasp of sexual specificity clearly becomes increasingly difficult. And although I have singled it out, *Rave Off* is by no means unique in positing the raver as a kind of non-specific generality. Tim Jordan's Deleuze and Guattari-informed interpretation of the rave as a 'Body without Organs', and Drew Hamment's reading of ravers as 'acid warriors' speak a similar language:

> The BwO of raving is the undifferentiated state that supports the connections that the rave-machine makes between its different elements. This undifferentiated state is a collective delirium produced by thousands of people jointly making the connections of drugs to dance, music to dance, dance to drugs, drugs to time, time to music and so on, and thereby gradually constructing the state of raving and so the BwO or raving. The delirium is non-subjective and smooth, as all the connections and functions of the machine give way to simple intensities of feeling. (Jordan, 1995, p. 130)

> Digital flows becoming corporeal, libidinal flows becoming cyber-sexual. In the dance digitality becomes organic: on the dancefloor the crowd switches on and becomes cyberpositive in the heterogenous unity of a prodigious new chromaticism. Libidinal flows

traverse the dancefloor, cultivating fractal patterns of shape, colour and emotion upon the mutating platform of the beat. A common pulse producing a polyphony of corporeal music; shouts and movements smearing the code, divergent energies united, synthesised by the drum pattern, and then spiralling off on new trajectories. (Hamment, 1995, p. 3)

Although these different interpretations might be thought-provoking, their failure to attend to specificities is a problem. It is extremely difficult to ground such readings in relation to the lived actualities of raving. Although I appreciate theoretically the many reasons why we might choose to loosen our hold on identity classifications – to stop interpellating subjects as sexed, and to thus challenge the positioning force of naming, I also realise how naïve and problematic it is to deny that such classifications continue to have very real effects. It is not, for example, particularly useful to consider rave as being the same thing for men and women. And it is at points like this that Thornton's work is so valuable. It reminds us that ravers come in different sexes. Moreover, and as I shall indicate later on, although raving can involve important feelings of having 'lost' oneself, it can also typically involve feelings of paranoia and intense self-consciousness. Again, all of this points to the need for more sustained and grounded examination of the specificities of particular actualisations of raving.

It is also a little suspicious perhaps, that just when practices traditionally associated with femininity (like dancing) come under the critical spotlight, this urge towards sexual neutering emerges. Sexual specificity simply cannot be ignored in the way that some of these theorists seem to suggest. This kind of neutering ignores the very important marking of the dancing female body as always already sexualised, different and 'other'. And although I agree that something about the rave context enables a radical loosening up of such associations, it is clearly still not the case that men and women within a rave are the same. For one thing, it is dangerous to wash over sex differences when it comes to the practicalities of raving. As Sue Lees reminds us, for example, women may now party as hard and as often as do their male counterparts, but 'the problem of getting home unscathed is a fear they routinely contend with' (1993: 5). Although the fact that quite often rave events do not finish until daylight (and for this reason many women feel safer getting home than they may once have done) questions about sexual safety are rarely absent from women's personal accounts of raving.

(iii) Innocence corrupted

Interestingly, the most obvious gendering of the raver came about in early 'panic' press reportage which fast established women as the 'victims' of rave, but just as quickly lost interest in them as the football 'thug' stepped to centre-stage of tabloid press focus. Girls and women were thus situated at the level of vulnerability by early press reports which stressed the idea of the endangered young woman. They were cast as what Sheila Henderson calls 'dancing damsels in the Acid House of distress' (1997: 66). Steve Redhead describes the situation very clearly:

> The potential victims in this tale of an evil cult, which the tabloids recounted, promptly materialised, as the generalities of 'youths', 'teenagers' and 'schoolchildren' gave way to specifically gendered subjects. *The Sun* on November 7 told how '14 year old Jenny' swallowed Ecstasy for the first time. *The Mirror* on the same day explained the way in which a 'young girl rolled a joint of cannabis' and how 'three young girls were spotted taking the mind-blowing drug LSD' and further, quoted one 17-year old girl claiming 'I had some Acid on me.' This portrayal of the typical Acid House victim as a young woman culminated in *The Sun* headline on November 24 of 'Acid fiends spike Page 3 girl's drink.' It was reported how Spanish men who were spiking girls' drinks 'would lie in wait and rape them' ... Women were thus established as the victims of deviance within the Acid House scene. (1993, p. 3)

'Victimised' women were soon dropped as figures of press interest. What replaced the endangered woman as a site of interest was, as Redhead points out, the newly emerging 'lager lout' who moved from the football terraces to the dance floor, bringing with him the threat of violence and disorder.

Female roles in narratives of contemporary club cultures

As this sketch of the discursive terrain surrounding rave and club cultures indicates, girls and women leave a very slight mark indeed.

Women do not feature centre-stage of Thornton's work because she is centrally interested in questions of a subcultural capital which is primarily the preserve of men. They receive scant attention from Redhead *et al* who tend to leave the raver ungendered, although Redhead himself does observe the extent to which rave 'victims' and 'demons' have been gendered by the British tabloid press. Finally, issues of femininity will be of little interest to those concerned with musical production and innovation, because women remain marginal at these levels. Arguably, what we therefore have before us in terms of club cultural criticism, is a manifold denial of women's presence within and experiences of contemporary social dance cultures. Yet hundreds of thousands of girls and women regularly rave. For many, such practices come to accumulate enormous and diverse significance. Failing to address such significance can, as I have repeatedly argued, mean that the study of today's dance cultures, ends up being a study of today's masculinities.

Indeed, one could be far more cynical about some strands of this state of play. We could ask for example, whether dance cultures have become interesting to Left scholars precisely *because* such large numbers of working-class *men* have become involved within them. It has, after all, long been the working-class man who has bestowed a certain 'credibility' on youth cultural movements, and who has been the most common focus of Left youth cultural critics, providing an anchor point for considerations of 'moral panics', youth 'resistance', cultural constructions of deviance, youthful innovations in the spheres of musical and cultural production, articulations of 'street' politics, and so forth. With rave, dance cultures have been largely de-feminised and also, wrenched from their traditional associations with male homosexuality – and maybe this is more significant than we admit. Perhaps it is just at the point when more working-class, 'straight' men get involved in dance cultures that these become worthy of the attentions of Left critics. Have dance cultures therefore become attention-worthy *not* because the dance floor has finally been recognised as a particularly significant site for the different constructions of the body and the world of which McClary writes, but rather because they now enable us to address familiar concerns about the cultural and political relations between 'authority' and working-class masculinity – because they enable us to speak a language we already know? Or has the social dance floor now become an interesting focus for study because it is being largely colonised by men who can momentarily absorb themselves in a space which has traditionally been seen as 'feminine', enjoy the experience, but nevertheless emerge with a sense of masculinity intact? Bradby for example, points out that the contemporary dancefloor has come to be seen as an enfolding, 'feminine' antidote to the alienation of contemporary British society (1993: 166). Men can now (without facing questions about their heterosexuality) lose themselves in the warm 'embrace' provided here. McRobbie also points out the extent to which men dancing on 'E':

> undergo a conversion to the soft, the malleable and the sociable rather than the anti-social, and through the almost addictive pleasure of dance they also enter into a different relationship with their own bodies, more tactile, more sensuous, less focussed around sexual gratification. (1994, p. 168)

Clearly, there is nothing wrong with the fact that raving men might undergo a momentary 'becoming feminine' (inasmuch as the sensuous and the soft are traditionally seen to be 'feminine'). The problem comes when this does so little to actually change the way that dance cultural histories are constructed, and where a situation continues in which boys and men are left with all of the leading roles within these histories. Raving masculinity may indeed undergo some kind of 'troubling' within a dance event, but when it comes to knowledge (be this academic or popular), male mastery remains very much intact. Hence, whilst the appeals, pleasures and significance of contemporary social dance cultures are often articulated in terms of some kind of 'loss' of identity, male 'authority' (be this the authority to speak 'knowledge' on behalf of dance cultures, or simply the authority to play the leading protagonists within dance cultural histories) remains very much alive. Bradby makes a similar point in referring to the 'death of the author' claims which appear to be fuelling much contemporary rock scholarship debate. She argues:

> But while it seems true that the old ideologies of authorship and creativity die hard, one could argue that they are kept alive especially by the 'expert' writing of the male rock press and among male groups and producers. (1993, p. 164)

Towards the specificities of raving subjects

Certain steps obviously need taking in order that we can shift our gaze away from the more familiar and attention-grabbing concerns which mark club cultural criticism, and direct it towards the significance of club cultural involvement for women.

First, we have to move beyond a dualistic resistance/conformity opposition which structures the focus of much traditional youth cultural scholarship. In the present case, this can tend to limit appraisal of dance cultures to either a celebration of youth's 'oppositionality', or a condemnation of its perceived conformity and leave us in the kind of position described by Nigel Thrift, who points to an interpretative framework whereby 'everything has to be forced into the dichotomy of resistance or submission and all of the paradoxical effects which cannot be understood in this way remain hidden' (1996: 2). Such a dichotomy dictates that a given cultural practice *can* be straightforwardly 'resistant' or wholly 'conservative'. In contrast to such views, Foucault's explication of the power/knowledge complex carries the welcome reminder that power and resistance are never wholly separate or mutually exclusive forces. Where there is power, so too is there resistance. The latter is never in a position of exteriority to power (Gordon, 1980).

Foucault's work raises important questions when it comes to the point of theorising a position of oppositionality. It emphasises that this can not be theorised as an abstract, but rather needs to be considered as always contingent and never complete. With respect to rave culture, it is therefore inadequate to equate raving (as some of the more celebratory commentary does) so unproblematically with 'autonomy' or with a resistance to 'meaning'. It is equally inadequate to conclude that just because men might dominate at the production side of this culture, it inevitably follows that women are always and only situated in a position of subordination. Small and specific acts of 'resistance' like grand and organised acts of domination and claims to truth, require closer scrutiny. These are never as stable or complete as they may appear.

A further problem with an oversimplistic attachment to the concept of 'resistance' concerns a failure to recognise its historical specificity. As George Lipsitz (1994) points out, all too often debate on contemporary youth cultures displays a continuing fixation with the 1960s and 1970s as an era of youth revolt. If hanging onto the concept of 'resistance' indicates a fixation with the 1960s and 1970s, then, and as I have suggested throughout, it also indicates a continuing fixation with the actions and experiences of young men.

Second, we have to keep club cultural criticism more firmly grounded in relation to specifics. The faceless 'mass' which commonly appears within this criticism needs, that is, to be given a more precise form in order that complexity, contradiction and diversity be made apparent. If we accept (despite the well-known difficulties with charting linear histories) that we can map a general objectivist history of contemporary club cultures – one based on the release of particular music tracks; the organisation of particular events; the development of particular musical technologies; the emergence in the popular press of 'demonic' drug-pushers and so on, then we can also look to how rave tells its stories through particular embodied experiences. Alongside other more objectivist foci then, specific embodied experiences can serve to keep debate alive, open and aware of diversity, rather than allowing it to become colonised by singular and singularising dominant narratives.

Third, we have to resist the kind of totalitarianism which very clearly underlies much existing club cultural criticism. By totalitarian I am referring to the assumption that club cultures *can* be reduced to, or read in terms of, a singular meaning structure. Hence, it is common to read of rave being ultimately, or at very least centrally, about one thing. In Thornton's case it is about an accumulation of subcultural capital. In others, it is about 'escape' (McRobbie, 1994): about 'meaninglessness' (Rietveld, 1993; Mellechi, 1993): about an ultimately 'free corporeal expression' (Sutcliffe, 1996): or about a Body without Organs (Jordan, 1995). Such totalitarianism is perhaps most surprising in the works collected within *Rave Off* because although many of these authors are intent on stressing the fundamental 'meaninglessness' of rave, this stress has precisely the opposite effect. It asserts that rave *is* fundamentally or essentially about a collapse of meaning. Hence, if it is at all useful to see rave (as these authors seem to suggest) as challenging totalising accounts of youth cultures, because it is about multiplicity, heterogeneity and fragmentation, then it does not seem particularly useful to simultaneously argue that rave can be reduced to a central or underlying feature. Clearly, the *Rave Off* contributors are not unique in this respect. Indeed, it has become very common to encounter commentary on rave which on the one hand celebrates its meaninglessness and resistance to definition, whilst on the other, asserts its underlying significance. Richard Sutcliffe for example, applauds rave's resistance to meaning, its challenge to totalising theories and its ability to evade surveillance, definition and regulation, whilst simultaneously claiming that rave is 'inherently' about autonomy (1996).

Viewing contemporary club cultures as essentially reducible to one thing is clearly problematic. Not only do such representations fail to engage with the complexities and diversity of these cultures, but they enable very oversimplistic value judgements to be made. So, in terms of their 'political' significance, contemporary club cultures are quite often read as being either 'positive' or 'negative', 'progressive' or 'retrogressive' and so forth. It should be obvious that within cultures so wide and varied as those which make up the contemporary social dance scene, there are bound to be both 'positive' and 'negative' cultural-political features, enabling possibilities and disempowering forcers, liberating potentials and oppressive tendencies, spaces for the explorations of radically 'alternative' subjectivities and instances in which existing social divisions are reinforced. In order that these sometimes contradictory features be made apparent, it is necessary to admit to the multiplicity of rave culture, and attend to the *different* ways in which ravers can come to make sense of this culture.

To reiterate and recap, we need to shift our focus. In order to see women's club cultural experiences as significant and an important subject matter for study, we need to move beyond the more visible levels of today's club cultures. Women tend not to be located at these levels, but to read-off from this fact the sexual-politics of rave is inadequate. Although the lack of sustained interest in femininity would seem to be justifiable on the grounds that club cultures are not *about* femininity, I have stressed that such an argument can be circular and self-fulfilling. Focus therefore needs to be more firmly shifted away from an interest in production, and towards questions of consumption. This involves challenging the view of club participants as the passive recipients of what might be a 'patriarchal' or capitalist ideology, or as compliant reflections of the structures of sociocultural production. As theorists like Richard Dyer (with reference to disco), Ien Ang (1985) and Charlotte Brunsdon (1978) – with reference to popular television and soap operas and Tania Modleski

(1984) and Janice Radway (1987) – with reference to romance fiction have, in their different ways, demonstrated, cultural participation and consumption within a capitalist and patriarchal context, cannot be assumed to straightforwardly reproduce or reinforce dominant powers. It cannot be known in advance what such a participation might mean to those involved.

Although works such as Radway's *Reading the Romance* and other feminist writings on popular cultural consumption have contributed much to the study of women's cultural usage, Ien Ang is correct to point out that such works often share a common political perspective based on an implicit assumption that women can benefit from some form of feminist consciousness raising. Here, the cultural product – the romance novel for instance – is seen as the 'function of a reformist goal; it is seen as a potential vehicle for teaching the mass of women who are not yet mobilised for feminist, emancipatory ideas' (1984, p. 656). Ang thus highlights a common problem with certain feminist works on popular cultural practice and consumption; it displays an implicit drive to read such practices as potentially progressive and as the embodiment of a latent feminist discontent which simply needs making explicit. Ang argues then, that there is something problematic about reading some underlying 'resistance' to superficially exploitative or oppressive practices. This needs to be borne in mind although for the purposes of the present project, where it comes to the situations and experiential accounts of clubbing women, it should not stop us from acknowledging what are sometimes quite explicit articulations of dissatisfaction with sex relations and what are views quite clearly echoing a popular 'feminism'. Although it is important to avoid oversimplistically viewing women's club cultural practices as 'resistant', it is equally important to hear challenge where this *is* being posed. Of course, this will never be all there is to say about such practices, and even explicit articulations of 'resistance' are often liable to be contradictory and partial.

Clearly, when it comes to rendering women's club cultural experiences and practices visible, feminist audience works such as the above can be inspiring. But because these are focused around women's 'in home' practices, their usefulness is limited. Clubbing and raving are significantly 'out of home' practices, engaged in at night and in spaces which are physically separate from the places and figures associated with authority and responsibility. Nonetheless, such works are important in their reluctance to write off cultural practices which superficially appear to be signs of oppression. Indeed, in writing about contemporary dance music and cultures, Bradby acknowledges the importance of such work, and points out that:

> the renewed interest in audience research in cultural studies has allowed a revalorisation of girls' and women's experience as fans of popular music and as creators of meaning in the music they listen to. (1993, p. 155)

It is however, Richard Dyer's analysis of disco which constitutes one of the most important interventions into dance cultural studies. As he argues, just because disco rests upon a capitalist mode of production, the way in which participants interact with, and make sense of this, cannot be assumed to echo capitalist sentiments:

> Cultural production under capitalism is necessarily contradictory and secondly, it may well be the case that capitalist cultural products are most likely to be contradictory at just those points – such as Disco – where they are most commercial and professional, where the urge to profit is at its strongest. Thirdly, this mode of cultural production has produced a commodity, Disco, that has been taken up by gays in ways that may well not have been intended by its producers. The anarchy of capitalism throws up commodities that an oppressed group can take up and use to cobble together its own culture. (1979, p. 12)

The same might be said of the ways in which women come to make sense of today's male-dominated social dance cultures. Although there is perhaps not such a recognisable 'girls' subculture within rave, there certainly *are* important discourses about female 'emancipation' coming to cohere around raving as a practice.

The variety of works which have shifted focus away from production and onto the lived experiences and consumption of popular culture have much to offer today's club cultural criticism. And works such as Helen Thomas's (1993) and Angela McRobbie's (1991) on the meanings that dance can carry for women, provide useful reminders of the importance of this shift. One way of getting at this importance is by attending to what women themselves actually make of and say about their practices. But this cannot be done in an 'innocent' way which would treat the experiential account as some kind of self-evident truth. The following chapter thus discusses some of the possibilities opened up by various poststructuralist feminisms for the development of a post-foundational study of experience and the personal narrative.

2
Situating Voices: towards a Post-Foundational Study of 'Women's Experiences'

For me there's nothing better. I feel completely safe and of course, you may get men giving you the eye but it really *is* entirely different to the club scenes I was involved in before. Something very important happened with rave and things have never gone back to what they were. It's the way that men and women behave towards each other. Mainly, like I said, I think it's because if you're in a dance event these days, you're there to *dance*. You're there to dance and not to pull. Everyone understands this and this is the greatest thing about it. Of course, you might *want* to pull and it's not out of the question, but something big is different and it spills into the outside world too. (Clare)

(Rave) was strikingly different to other club scenes. There was no alcohol around, so little aggression and little emphasis on chatting people up, and the cattle-market element of say disco didn't seem to be around. (Ann)

Rave is a completely different scene. Men seem very unaggressive. They're friendly in a completely different way from people being friendly when they're completely pissed-up. The men – even in the kind of hard-core clubs – aren't sort of predatory, and they're not there to pull. (Amy)

Gender and sexual politics are areas where overexcited and unsupported claims for the radicalism of dance music culture are commonly heard. (Hesmondhalgh, 1995, p. 9)

> Moreover, although raves are supposed to be 'sexless' affairs –
> that is, clothing is unisex and participants are not there to
> get laid – it does not follow that they are necessarily sexually
> progressive. (Thornton, 1996, p. 56)

> We can in no way be certain therefore, that the broader
> changing climate of sexual politics is reflected in rave.
> (McRobbie, 1994, p. 168)

This juxtaposition of statements illustrates some significantly different and more importantly, differently privileged, knowledges about rave culture. I open this chapter with such a 'montage' bearing in mind Walter Benjamin's belief in the radical potential of juxtaposition for rupturing or disturbing the continuum of the world. As James Rolleston puts it, in discussing Benjamin, 'passages from different kinds of text speak on a new level when juxtaposed' (1989, p. 16). Locating female ravers' voices alongside those of academic commentators serves here to lay the ground for the central questions around which this chapter is structured. How can these non-academic women's voices be rendered culturally significant? And how can the kinds of experiences voiced by these women be made to signify as anything other than 'mistakes', signs of a kind of 'false' consciousness, or murmurs of a groundless Utopianism?

In the previous chapter, I concentrated upon some of the forces which appear to work in directing attention away from the place, practices and experiences of women within contemporary club cultures. In the present chapter, I want to build on this suggestion in addressing a further set of problems which face us as academic theorists attempting to take seriously women's experiential accounts. These problems relate to our situation within a poststructuralist climate, wherein the categories of 'experience', 'women' and 'reality' are all being so radically troubled. The first and perhaps the most important issue which presents itself in a study such as this one, thus concerns the status that women's experiential claims are afforded; how these are mobilised and indeed, what it means to speak of 'women' as a category. Angela McRobbie has recently approached some such questions in arguing for the strategic use within cultural studies of what she calls the 'three Es'; the empirical, the ethnographic and the experiential (1997a). An unquestioned embrace of the 'anti-Es' (anti-essentialism, poststructuralism and psychoanalysis) can, as McRobbie rightly argues, itself run the risk of cementing a new poststructuralist faith or foundation. Moreover, such an embrace can leave us with few, if any, ways to approach the actual lived practices and experiences of embodied cultural subjects. We are left worried about essentialism, nervous about making truth-claims, anxious about not wanting to present ourselves as 'representatives', unsure about the status of individual experience, and sceptical about those processes whereby we can end up constructing the very subjects we claim to be describing. As she puts it:

> At every point the spectre of 'humanism' haunts the practice of those who align themselves with the 'anti-Es'. Ethnography? That truth-seeking activity reliant on the (often literary) narratives of exoticism and difference? Can't do it, except as a deconstructive exercise. Empiricism? The 'representation' of results, the narrative of numbers? Can't do it either, except as part of a critical genealogy of sociology and its role in the project of modernity and science. Experience? That cornerstone of human authenticity, that essential core of individuality, the spoken voice as evidence of being and the coincidence of consciousness with identity? Can't do it other than as a psychoanalytic venture. (1997a, p. 171)

McRobbie is entirely correct in giving voice to the sense of hopelessness we can sometimes feel as academic feminists wanting to say something positive – rather than wanting simply to continue the deconstructive and self-interrogatory tendencies encouraged by various poststructuralist teachings. What her argument clearly and convincingly suggests however, is that we can *know* the nerves, *feel* the anxieties, *experience* the insecurities and *still* do research on the lived experiences of sexed subjects. It is not only that we *can*, but – as feminists – we *must* find ways of connecting 'theoretical' insights to popular cultural practice and discourse. This is not simply because some of the theoretical detours which certain poststructuralism urges us towards, can take us so very far away from the lived actualities of 'real' subjects, but also because there is something very problematic about the push to have us relinquish our hold on identity categories, and our interest in actual subjects-in-culture, just at that point when many previously silenced groups are only now coming to find a voice and to construct an 'identity' for themselves. McRobbie therefore calls for new and challenging ways to think about how 'culture' in the general relates to the everyday practices of particular subjects-in-context, or what in an earlier work, she calls, 'identities-in-culture' (1992, p. 730).

Several important issues have to be tackled or at very least addressed however, before we can return to talk about identity, experience and knowledge. Poststructuralism and psychoanalysis have raised challenging and difficult questions about 'truth', self-presence, identity and knowledge. How then, are we to formulate a model through which we can consider women's experiences as non-innocent, non-identical and partial? What follows constitutes a brief exploration of what a feminist post-foundational (and in this respect poststructuralist) study of 'women's experience' might entail, and it owes a lot to the work which McRobbie has already put into thinking about new ways of reinserting the field of 'lived experience' back into cultural studies. It is by no means a thorough review of the development of poststructuralist theorisations of identities-in-culture. Instead, it is an address of some of the *specific* questions which a project such as this one throws up, or the *particular* hurdles which appear to need clearing, before we can actually get round to con-sidering the experiential accounts of raving women. Drawing selectively from work by Donna Haraway (1991), Rosi Braidotti (1994), Stuart Hall (1996), and Valerie Walkerdine (1997), the chapter addresses several interrelated questions:

1) What use is the category of 'women' within our poststructuralist climate?
2) What status can the experiential account have within this climate? and,
3) On what grounds can our academic claims to knowledge now rest?

But, and to reiterate, it is McRobbie's work on the 'Es' and the 'anti-Es' which provides the major framework through which these questions are approached, because it constitutes one of the best and clearest attempts at outlining how theory can actually be connected to con-temporary research practice. Rather than reiterating her arguments however, I simply want to call upon them in giving form to the treatment of 'women' and of the experiential account in the present project.

'Women'? Thinking beyond closure

Perhaps one of the most pressing questions facing poststructuralist feminist theory and politics today, concerns how to speak of 'women', and 'women's experiences' without denying differences between women, and without resorting to a form of essentialism. There are, as I have stressed throughout, a number of important reasons for keeping a grasp of the category of 'women'. Not least of all is the fact that postmodern and poststructuralist deconstructions of the auth- orial individual *can* mean that subjects who are only now gaining the *right* to claim an identity, are being urged to let go of this illusory search for coherence, and to embrace instead, fragmentation and incompleteness. Hence, those (like women) who had the most *need* and *reason* to challenge liberal humanist models of the 'individual' are now being attacked for their own insistence upon the sexual specificity of the subject, and criticised because such an insistence appears to involve a denial of differences *between* women. As Barbara Bradby puts it:

> The 'death of the subject', to which feminism has in no small part contributed, was turned back on it as the sin of 'essentialism', and the pioneering feminist theory of barely a decade before castigated for its naive belief that all women share common characteristics (1993, p. 157)

Bradby thus highlights the risk that the challenge to liberal humanism (which in its feminist form, sought to expose the gender specificity of the 'human') runs of leading to an abandonment of sexually specific categories altogether. She is therefore critical of those theor- etical moves which invite us as feminists to *unproblematically* accept the fragility of 'identity' and of women's 'reality', and asserts that such moves make her:

> ... want to revert to gender generalizations and question why *for women* reality needs to be any *more* unstable and disorderly than it already is. (1993, p. 158)

She continues:

> Part of women's 'invisible' oppression is surely the way in which
> we must 'cope' in our persons not only with the instability of our
> own fragmented roles, but with clearing up the disorder of others
> on a daily basis. The point is surely to make *this* reality even more
> apparent, to dislodge from centre stage the 'reality' of an automat-
> ically functioning social order which it has been men's privilege
> to believe. (1993, p. 158)

What Bradby therefore alerts us to is the fact that earlier feminist
challenges to liberal humanist conceptions of the author, and to the
'unsituated' truth-claims which have traditionally posed as *the* truth,
need not be viewed as an incitement to reject the concept of 'reality'
per se. Rather (although she does not use the exact language
herself), such critiques are best viewed as demands that knowledge
be 'situated' – cognizant of its own standpoint and honest about its
own partiality. As Haraway (1991) reminds us, just because we
accept that we cannot know *everything*, this does not mean that we
can know *nothing*. This kind of resignation is, she suggests, only
likely to occur if we were ever *in* the position to entertain the idea
that we *could* know everything. The standpoints of the subjugated
are less likely to be troubled by the collapse of this fallacy. And they
do not therefore require challenge in the same way as do those
knowledges which claim to come from 'nowhere while claiming to
see everything comprehensively'. This is not to view subjugated
knowledges as 'innocent' but rather, to recognise that they are less
likely to:

> allow denial of the critical and interpretative core of all know-
> ledge. They are savvy to modes of denial through repression,
> forgetting, and disappearing acts – ways of being nowhere while
> claiming to see everything comprehensively. The subjugated have
> a decent chance to be on to the god-trick and all its dazzling –
> and therefore, blinding – illuminations. 'Subjugated' standpoints
> are preferred because they seem to promise more adequate, sus-
> tained, objective, transforming accounts of the world. (1990,
> p. 191)

There is something clearly very problematic then, with viewing earlier feminist demands to 'situate' knowledge and truth-claims as calls for a rejection, *in principle*, of the concept of 'reality'.

To return to the project of researching women, it seems important that we do not allow calls for the 'situation' of knowledge to prevent us from generating any kind of (albeit partial) knowledge at all. It is equally important, that work which has stressed the fragmentary make-up of sexed identity, and which has emphasized the fact that all identity is constituted partly within fantasy, is not allowed to become a complete barrier to actually doing grounded work *as*, and *with*, women. Bradby is clearly not alone in challenging the ways in which we are invited – as women researching women – to question the bases of our work. McRobbie, for example, also points out that:

> Having only recently achieved some degree of institutional recognition in the academy, the experience of being robbed of this authority and of being challenged as to whether it is possible to speak in this context 'as a woman' is unlikely to be met with a wholly friendly welcome. (1997a, p. 186)

What both Bradby and McRobbie thus point to are the problems (and the inequalities) involved in forcing female identity and 'reality' into question, just because male 'reality' is finally being troubled and shifted from centre stage.

Whilst we might remain reluctant to give up speaking *about* and *as* 'women', we are also all too aware that the category can serve as a means of appropriating others and of denying heterogeneity. For this reason, contemporary theorists such as Donna Haraway and Rosi Braidotti are centrally engaged in refiguring ways of talking about 'women' and 'women's experience', whilst avoiding the homogenising and appropriating effects that such classifications can have. Haraway thus argues for a politics of difference, but stresses that 'experience like difference is about contradictory and necessary connection' (1991, p. 109). Such a politics is not to be confused with a type of subjectivist relativism or a form of liberal humanism. Instead, it should search to find new ways of simultaneously articulating collectivity and multiplicity. In her own words:

> For the complex category and even more complex people called
> 'women', *A* and *not-A* are likely to be simultaneously true. This
> correct exaggeration insists that even the simplest matters in femi-
> nist analysis require contradictory moments and a wariness of
> their resolution, dialectically or otherwise. 'Situated Knowledges'
> is a shorthand term for this insistence. (1991, pp. 110–11)

Similarly, Braidotti, in envisaging a new way of speaking about, and
identifying with, the category of 'woman' argues:

> In feminist theory one *speaks* as a woman, although the subject
> 'woman' is not a monolithic essence defined once and for all but
> rather the site of multiple, complex, and potentially contradictory
> sets of experiences defined by overlapping variables such as class,
> race, age, lifestyle, sexual preference and others. (1994, p. 4)

One of the values of both Haraway's and Braidotti's work is that it
encourages us to continue feminist work, whilst reminding us that
our situated accounts are, like those of the subjects and groups we
research, partial and open to contestation. A feminist poststructuralism
thus involves refiguring the category of 'women' so that it speaks of
difference and also of the temporary nature of what Hall calls the
'suturing effects' of subject/structures of meaning relations. Valerie
Walkerdine's work on young girls stresses this fantasmatic aspect of
identification. In writing about the categories of femininity and masculinity, she suggests one way of moving beyond the essentialism
which much feminist work has come to be accused of:

> I am suggesting that femininity and masculinity are fictions linked
> to fantasies deeply embedded in the social world which can take
> on the status of fact when inscribed in the powerful practices, like
> schooling, through which we are regulated. (1990, p. xiv)

Walkerdine stresses the incompleteness of fictions of femininity, arguing that such fictions do not entirely work in guaranteeing coherence:

> Is there an authentic female voice? For me the answer lies not, as
> some feminists have suggested, in some kind of essential feminine
> voice that has been silenced, but in that which exists in the inter-

stices of our subjugation. We can tell other stories . . . The stories of our subjugation do not tell the whole truth: our socialization does not work. (Ibid.)

Recognising the 'messiness' of feminist research does not have to mean giving up. And such a recognition should not be allowed to become yet another means by which certain groups are denied a voice and presence within cultural studies. It can simply mean a strategic foundationalism; a move which involves prioritising sexual difference in the recognition of both differences, and what Haraway calls the 'just-barely-possible connections' among women (1990: 113). As Braidotti argues:

Speaking as a female feminist entails that priority is granted to issues of gender or, rather, of sexual difference in the recognition of differences among women. (1994, p. 4)

Acknowledging multiplicity and difference should not therefore, lead us to an abandonment of the category of 'women' altogether. What is required is precisely the opposite. Instead of ditching the category *because* of difference, we need to redefine it *in terms* of such diversity. This is not about embracing endless difference, or about celebrating the idiosyncratic make-up of individual subjects. In the present study, it is about charting both the connections and the contradictions between the different experiential accounts of a group of raving women. And although I am aware of the extent to which I might be constructing the very group I claim to be talking about (and I shall return to this shortly), this is a group which is, in many respects, *already* situated as distinct or different in relation to contemporary club cultures. It is a group which tends *not* to accumulate clubbing subcultural capital in the same way as a male group would; which tends *not* to be associated with the sociocultural production of these cultures; which tends *not* to be thought of in terms of 'expertise', and which presents very different questions when it comes to issues of sexual and personal safety, domestic responsibility and culturally specific notions about 'appropriate' sexed being. These factors alone provide ample reason for recognising raving women as a distinct or different category, although this difference clearly does not say *all* that could be said about any given individual or group. And it does not tell us about how a given subject will negotiate a positionality in relation to this larger situation. Structural, social, and sexual factors may well mark women within dance cultures as different, but how actual women deal with, negotiate and live this 'marking' requires closer attention. One way of attending to such negotiations comes, as I have repeatedly stressed, from looking to the experiential accounts of different raving women.

Experience? Thinking beyond humanism

But a feminist poststructuralist consideration of the experiential account can no longer speak the 'innocent' language of humanism. As McRobbie rightly notes, the experiential account has traditionally been seen as reflecting a 'true self'. It has been understood as the cornerstone of truth about the subject. A feminist poststructuralist return to the experiential account must, then, involve the recognition that such accounts are never complete and neither are they expressions of a fully formed and coherent human 'individual'. As McRobbie puts it, in outlining the problems with earlier feminist work on girls' and women's cultural practices:

> The spoken testimony of girls and women was here taken as expressive of a full human being, rather than understood as partial, fragmented, articulations of available language codes. (1997a, p. 172)

What is required then, is precisely this recognition that experiential accounts are partial. They do not represent a 'full human subject' and neither are they about representations which are somehow 'uncontaminated' by language, culture and context more broadly. But, as McRobbie explains, this recognition does not have to be met with resignation:

> But just because experience comes as a pre-packaged set of practices while disguising itself as what is unique and most true about ourselves, this does not mean it cannot find a place in feminist cultural studies. (1997a, p. 184)

Perhaps its place comes in terms of its status as what Haraway (drawing on de Lauretis) calls 'a semiosis: an embodying of meaning'. The experiential account can therefore be considered, not as evidence of a subject's core personhood, but rather in terms of how culturally and historically specific narratives (including contemporary narratives which construct us as 'feeling' and psychologised selves) are worked through by a given subject, and called upon in making sense of the world. Attending to the experiential account, can then, provide a way into examining a given subject's attachments to particular narratives. It is not enough that we chart contextually and historically specific cultural discourses. We need to develop ways of exploring how the subject performs in relation to these discourses. In writing about identities, Stuart Hall borrows from Stephen Heath the concept of 'suturing' to get at the ways in which the subject is hailed by, and invests in, available subject positions. As he puts it:

> The notion that an effective suturing of the subject to a subject-position requires, not only that the subject is 'hailed', but that the subject invests in this position, means that suturing has to be thought of as an articulation, rather than a one-sided process, and that in turn, puts identification, if not identities firmly on the academic agenda. (1996, p. 6)

Working with experiential accounts can provide one way of examining this two-way process.

In calling for a return to 'lived experience', McRobbie rightly points out that the value of this is that it allows for:

> A form of investigation where the impact and significance of empirical changes in culture and in society on living human subjects can be observed and analysed and where these same human subjects are invited to reflect on how they live through and make sense of such changes. (1997, p. 170)

The experiential account can therefore be called upon in examining the available subject positions which invite or hail the subject; positions whose occupancy is never total but always fragmented, and partly based upon fantasmatic identifications. Working with women's experiential accounts does not therefore, *have* to be about mobilising such experiences in the construction of a sealed category of sameness, and it does not *have* to be about viewing the experiential account as an innocent reflection of a subject's coherent or total 'interior' make-up. Rather, such accounts can inform us of the available fictions of femininity which circulate within a given culture at a given time, and more importantly, how individual women negotiate a relationship with and make sense of these fictions. Through attending to these individual negotiations, the just-barely-possible connections of which Haraway speaks can be made explicit. As she puts it:

> Women's studies must negotiate a very fine line between appropriation of another's (never innocent) experience and the delicate construction of just-barely-possible affinities and just-barely-possible connections that might just make a difference in local and global histories.' (1991, p. 113)

This new politics then, is pitched against the essentialising and homogenising tendencies of some earlier forms of feminism. It is about finding new ways of speaking, which are not about closure or appropriation. As Braidotti puts it, in envisaging the mapping of connections, links and affinities between women:

> Drawing a flow of connections need not be an act of appropriation. On the contrary, it marks transitions between communicating states or experiences. (1994, p. 5)

A post-foundational treatment of 'women's experience', therefore, has to work against the kind of colonisation involved in earlier embraces of subjects into some kind of 'sisterhood' of shared experience; something which, as McRobbie points out, is a 'phantasmatic signifier', a Utopian projection, guaranteed to disappoint. We need therefore, to work with 'women', not as a unified category, but as a class of fragile partnerships. She argues therefore:

> On a more pragmatic level, we have to live with the fragility of such partnerships rather than waiting for a future where unity is somehow miraculously achieved. (1997a, p. 185)

Working with women's experiential accounts does not therefore, mean that we have to see ourselves as searching for, or dealing with, some fundamental essence. Neither does it mean that we should view such accounts as total, or as expressive of a full and coherent individual.

Knowledge, partiality, situation: thinking beyond the 'god-trick'

If poststructuralism invites us to rethink how and why we call, as feminists, upon the category of 'women' and 'women's experience', then by definition, it forces us towards a greater self-reflexivity. Central to a post-foundational feminist politics then, is a constant awareness of the dangers of constructing the very subjects and 'realities' we claim to be talking about. Haraway's and Braidotti's work carry constant reminders of the need to make connections rather than closures, to map affinities rather than searching for all-encompassing categories, and to touch rather than appropriate. As Braidotti puts it: 'Drawing a flow of connections need not be an act of appropriation. On the contrary, it marks transitions between communicating states or experiences.' (1994, p. 5)

Their emphasis on the potential engendered by making such connections, gives Braidotti's and Haraway's work an optimistic and enabling quality which we can easily overlook if we continue 'beating ourselves up' about our 'power over', and our ability to construct, those we speak about. I understand and accept that I construct the women I have researched as women of a *particular* kind. In my defence however, and to give at least some acknowledgement to these women's active participation in the whole process of their construction as 'raving women', these are women who were themselves actively involved in, and recognised themselves within, my own interpellation of, or invitation to, 'women clubbers'. As I explain in the following chapter, the present interviewees came forward either because they had heard of my work and recognised themselves within this, or because they had read the following flier.

ATTENTION – WOMEN

I am a student at Goldsmiths College and am doing research into girls' and women's experiences of various club scenes. I am exploring what these experiences say about femininity in the '90s. My major concerns at present are to look at how women experience and

---

Box – *continued*

understand activities such as social dance, social drug-use and clubbing. I want to pay particular attention to whether practices such as clubbing (and all that goes with it) allow us to develop different views of ourselves as women.

At the moment, I am trying to contact women who are interested in being interviewed, and who feel they have something to say on this topic. If you have one or two hours to spare, I can either call at your home, arrange to meet you somewhere, or invite you to come to Goldsmiths College. Interviews will be unstructured and pretty informal. Basically, you will be asked to talk about what you feel you get out of clubbing, which kinds of clubs you prefer and why, and how you feel clubbing 'fits' with your identity as a 'woman'.

I am also keen to interview women in groups, so if you'd rather make it a group thing, that's fine. All information is strictly confidential and all names will be changed when this work is written up.

Although this is maybe a somewhat seductive invite to women to construct/recognise themselves not only as 'ravers', but as actual sources of knowledge, I do not view this as problematic. Instead, I see it as facilitating some kind of 'flow of connections' in the way that Braidotti talks about these. *Someone*'s got to make the first move; put the chain in motion. And although not all interviewees were contacted after responding to this flier, all of the interviewees *did* volunteer because they somehow recognised themselves in this invite. In fact, I was incredibly surprised by just how easy it was to find interviewees. So, something was obviously 'out there' before *I* came along.

As feminists, we have rightly come to take questions about our status and power very seriously. As academics involved in the 'political' project of writing and speaking about others, this is inevitable. But there is something a little problematic about over-inflated ideas about 'our' own importance and 'our' role in constructing the world and others within this. This is something I have learnt very clearly over the course of my own research. For me, it now makes far more sense to speak of strategic, political and always self-reflexive intervention, rather than to remain fixated upon 'our' power to construct the world. Such a fixation can betray a form of arrogance on the part of us, as academics. Of course, our representations are interpretations. All representation is.

Of course, we sometimes have a greater degree of cultural capital attached to our claims to truth than do our research subjects. But this is not *always* the case. Indeed, working in a field such as mine, I was far more likely to have my *subcultural* rather than my *cultural* capital questioned. In short, very rarely did I feel like some socially 'superior' academic coming into the lives of 'ordinary folk'. Sometimes we have 'power' and sometimes we don't. Sometimes our academic claims are afforded a certain authority, and sometimes they aren't. Sometimes (and despite our efforts to avoid it) our interpretations might offend those we speak about. And sometimes these others simply do not care or are just not interested. Indeed, the academic researcher (like the research subject) can be made to feel 'inferior'.

The unidirectional 'power over' model of the research encounter is clearly limited. Power works *between* subjects, within contexts. My own experience for example, was one of having been as 'constructed' by my subjects as they were by me. The interviews involved ongoing negotiations of very different positionalities. Some women appeared slightly amused by my work and by the fact that I was being funded to research their practices. One, although she volunteered to be interviewed, voiced an explicit dislike of academics who were trying to 'get off' on 'other people's lives'. Others treated me as if I did have some great authority (and this was particularly obvious when I turned up to one group interview and the women said that they were really surprised that I wasn't wearing a suit). Others situated me as a kind of political ally. One in particular, Louise (who is involved in the Rainbow Party Alliance), saw our meeting as a means of furthering both of our projects. She has thus remained in frequent contact, informing me of her organised dance parties, and more recently of her involvement in local politics. Some participants were keen to read the final work, whilst others were clearly interested in no more than talking to me. In some situations I felt challenged as to my credentials as a 'raver'. In others, I was positioned as a 'sister' out to celebrate 'girl power'. Several interviewees invited me to rave with them, whilst with others I had no further involvement. Most situations felt relaxed, 'safe' and pretty casual. One felt like the complete opposite. Here a young woman spoke excitedly and at great length about her club cultural experiences, but repeatedly (and nervously) reminded me throughout that if her male lover showed up, I would have to hide the recorder and pretend to be someone else. Her lover would, she said, 'kill her', if he heard what she was saying. He did turn up and we did hide the recorder. I came away from this interview feeling very differently about my work. It left me confused. Was I being irresponsible? Voyeuristic? Should I include the interview, even though the woman's name was changed? I asked her about how sure she was before leaving. She assured me that she wanted to be included and even invited me back to do another interview.

The point is that the workings of 'power' within the research situation are never straightforward. I interviewed women, reconstructed them as particular kinds of subjects and reworked their (already partial) accounts en route. But I always remained aware of this. And I have personally not gone through this period with a neat, coherent and comfortable self intact. Lawrence Grossberg sums up what the whole research process felt like to me, because he sees this as a process of connections rather than as a project of appropriation or colonisation of another's reality:

> Intellectuals do not construct reality, any more than do everyday subjects. Cultural critics are co-travellers and, within the limited possibilities available to us at any moment, we have our role to play. (1988, p. 388)

A poststructuralist feminist approach to the 'three Es' has, then, to see itself as forwarding the mapping of affinities between (always partial and potentially contradictory) situations.

Conclusions

I have argued for the need for more empirical work within cultural studies, and within club cultural studies in particular. As McRobbie stresses:

> Doing empirical work need not mean becoming an out-and-out empiricist. And given the low profile that empirical research has had in cultural studies over the last 20 years, what this might mean now, in the late 1990s, is not just beginning to do empirical

work informed by questions which emerge from a poststructuralist paradigm (for example, exploring the diverse and fluid subjectivities of 'young women'), it might also mean quite simply strategically (or opportunistically) speaking the language of empiricism as and when required. (1997a, p. 183)

We cannot allow some of the challenges posed by poststructuralism to prevent us from making positive statements about actual identities-in-culture. Instead, we have to work *with* such challenges and build out of them, a way of working which enables us to do something new and different. The critiques which have come out of poststructuralism force us to find new ways of thinking about how we research others, and how we come to understand our own situations in relation to the knowledges we produce. Such new ways must, as I have repeatedly stressed, involve an acknowledgement of our own situation and by extension, of the partiality of our own vision. As Haraway points out in relation to the production of 'situated knowledges':

> So not so perversely, objectivity turns out to be about particular and specific embodiment, and definitely not about the false vision promising transcendence of all limits and responsibility. The moral is simple: only partial perspective promises objective vision . . . Feminist objectivity is about limited location and situated knowledge, not about transcendence and splitting of subject and object. In this way we might become answerable for what we learn how to see. (1991, p. 190)

Although I have pointed to the kind of hopelessness we can experience as feminist researchers within our contemporary climate, there is clearly another side to this story. If there is a sense of hopelessness, then there is also a real sense of promise as well. Particularly through the work of Haraway and Braidotti, comes a clear and welcome sense of optimism about our potential for doing something new as feminists. As Haraway puts it:

> We are bound to seek perspective from those points of view, which can never be known in advance, which promise something quite extraordinary, that is knowledge potent for constructing worlds less organized by axes of domination. (1991, p. 113)

In formulating new feminist visions of the world, these theorists set out to construct what Braidotti (in talking about her figure of the 'nomad') describes as: 'The kind of critical consciousness that resists settling into socially coded modes of thought and behaviour' (1994, p. 5).

Both Braidotti and Haraway seek to challenge the oversimplistic division between fact and fiction which, in the past, has limited our address of the visionary aspects of politics. Their feminist figurations are, as Braidotti makes clear, as much about 'imaginations' and 'visions' as they are about political action. As she argues:

> I feel the need for a qualitative leap of the feminist political imagination. I believe in the empowering force of the political fictions that are proposed by feminists as different from each other as Luce Irigaray and Donna Haraway. (1994, p. 3)

The work which Braidotti and Haraway have carried out on new feminist figurations constitutes a radically challenging and empowering move beyond any easy fact/fiction division. It refuses any easy split between the visionary and the 'objective'. As Constance Penley puts it, in describing Haraway's work on feminist figurations, this:

> Paradoxically both describes . . . a new, actually existing, hybrid subjectivity and offers a polemical, Utopian vision of what new subjectivities ought to be, or will be. In other words, it's something actually existing now but also an image. (1991, p. 8)

Such figurations offer a positive move forward in affording us ways of understanding what our work can actually constitute. They are called upon here, not simply in acknowledging the present study's status as a situated 'fiction', but also as a way of making sense of interviewee's own claims; claims which, it is argued, both describe new and actually existing subjectivities *and* speak of as-yet unrealised images or visions of the world. To once again cite Bradby:

> The musical power of the disenfranchised – whether youth, the underclass, ethnic minorities, women or gay people – more often resides in their ability to articulate different ways of construing the body, ways that bring along in their wake the potential for different experiential worlds. (1993, p. 34)

The 'worlds' of which Bradby writes, are not ones that we can necessarily *touch*. They are, I believe, both actual, *and* partly constituted within a collective 'imagination', or as part of a collective 'vision' of the as-yet unknown. We need a way then, of understanding these worlds as both actually existing spaces, *and* as visionary constructions of the *what-could-be*, or *what-should-be*. Likewise, we need new ways of understanding raving women's claims about such 'worlds'; ways which allow us to see both the actualities *and* the visions and desires, which inform these claims. This is not about turning away from the 'real'. Rather, it is about finally accepting the visionary and the imaginary as part and parcel of how we make sense of our worlds. As Haraway reminds us:

> The imaginary and the rational – the visionary and objective vision – hover close together ... Science has been Utopian and visionary from the start; that is one reason 'we' need it. (1991, p. 192)

McRobbie has recently written about what she calls 'a semi-structure' of feminist feeling in the culture of today's young women. She writes:

> By exploring the climate of change in the culture of young women today, one is tapping into something which exists in a state of disaggregated latency, a 'semi-structure' of feeling, to re-phrase Raymond Williams, which surfaces at unexpected moments in unexpected ways. (1997b, p. 159)

We need to find ways, I am arguing, of speaking about this semi-structure of feminist feeling; this state of 'disaggregated latency'. The new feminist figurations which Haraway and Braidotti construct, provide one way of thinking not simply about the material conditions of everyday life, but also the stories, fantasies and 'semi-structures' of feeling which saturate and give meaning to these conditions. Viewing interviewee accounts in these terms enables me to foreground the extent to which they speak as much about desires for a future as they do about present circumstances. This involves acknowledging the imaginary and visionary qualities of such accounts and the addressing not simply of that which goes on in the social *body*, but also that which goes on within the social *imaginary*.

The kind of contemporary feminist theory which I am most interested in then, suggests not only new directions for feminist research, but also new ways of thinking about subjectivity and about the status of our own claims to knowledge. It promises something new, and aims at creating alternative interpretative frameworks and ways of seeing. As Braidotti puts it:

> The term figuration refers to a style of thought that evokes or expresses ways out of the phallocentric vision of the subject. A figuration is a politically informed account of an alternative subjectivity. I feel a real urgency to elaborate alternative accounts, to learn to think differently about the subject, to invent new frameworks, new images, new modes of thought. (1994, p. 1)

As Haraway points out in describing what she sees as a new successor science, 'faithful' accounts of the 'real' necessarily involve engagement with the visionary:

> I think Harding's plea for a successor science and for postmodern sensibilities must be read to argue that this close touch of the fantasmatic element of hope for transformative knowledge and the severe check and stimulus of sustained critical inquiry are jointly the ground of any believable claim to objectivity or rationality not riddled with breath-taking denials and repressions. (1991, p. 192)

And as Valerie Walkerdine rightly argues:

> The building up of something new is so much more difficult than the act of taking the existing truths apart. But in my view, we must begin to try to build things. This building will not be easy and we are bound to make lots of mistakes, but surely it is in the act of attempting to move forward that we find our way...In *Structure, Sign and Play*, Derrida ((1978) in Walkerdine, 1997) sets out the conundrum in terms of a metaphor of birth: 'Here there is a kind of question, let us still call it historical, whose conception, formation, gestation and labour we are only catching a glimpse of today. I employ these words, I admit, with a glance toward those who, in a society from which I do not exclude myself, throw their

eyes away when faced by the as yet unnameable which is proclaiming itself and which can do so, as is necessary whenever a birth is in the offing, only under the species of the nonspecies, in the formless, mute, infact, and terrifying form of monstrosity...'. I think we are giving birth to no less than a different way of working and the more of us push together the easier that birth will become. There is always pain attached to birth and very often complications, but all of this pales beside the wonder of a new life in the making. (1997, p. 62)

We must work with the enabling possibilities for new kinds of work which poststructuralism opens up, rather than resigning ourselves, or giving up simply because we accept the situation and partiality of our visions and knowledges.

Part II of this project constitutes an attempt at drawing a flow of connections, (without disrespecting differences), between the experiential accounts of a group of raving women.

Part II

From Bedroom Culture to Dance Cultures

Introduction: Down to Specifics: Study Design, Method and Presentation

Eighteen women took part in this study. These women were contacted after responding to adverts given out between 1992 and 1994 at a variety of (both free and charged) London-based dance events.[1] Alternatively, interviewees contacted me between 1990 and 1994 having heard about my research from people whom I had already interviewed or from colleagues and friends. Although I had believed that leafleting would prove to be the most successful means of contacting potential participants, it was actually through word-of-mouth that I ended up meeting most of these women. Although six women contacted me after reading a leaflet, only four of these (one individual and one group of three) were able to make an interview appointment. The remaining 13 participants came to hear of my project through other people.[2]

The first four interviews were conducted individually with Miriam, Catherine, Ann and Elaine all of whom were interviewed as part of an M.A. research project on women and the early British rave scene, and all of whom volunteered for interview, having heard about my research interests through either friends or colleagues. All of the other women were interviewed as part of my PhD research and it is mainly upon these interviews (because they were part of the much longer and more in-depth project) that I will be concentrating – although Catherine, Miriam, Ann and Elaine will also be referenced where relevant. The first phase of interviews conducted as part of this longer project was carried out with Louise (who contacted me after reading a leaflet she had received at the first anti-CJB demonstration held in Trafalgar Square), Jane (who had heard about my work through a friend and who wanted to talk to me), and Amy (whose phone number was given to me by a man I had met through previous research, and who believed that she would like to talk about her experiences, and particularly about her experiences of aging in relation to her clubbing practices). Louise was interviewed in her work place, and both Jane and Amy were interviewed in their homes.

Having carried out, transcribed and studied these interviews, I moved onto my next phase. This involved individual interviews with Clare, Teresa and Michelle, and one group interview with Holly, Anna and Kerry. Amy had given me Clare's contact details, suggesting that she would probably be an interesting interviewee because rave culture had become very central to her social life. I contacted her and we arranged to meet in her home. Teresa contacted me having been given my number by a friend who knew of my work. Again I arranged to interview her in her home. I interviewed Michelle with a colleague Tiziana Terranova who was doing work on the Advance Party. Michelle was a founder of the movement and was at the time squatting in part of North London University, where the interview took place.[3] Holly, Kerry and Anna had heard about my research through a fellow academic. I contacted the women and arranged a group interview in one of their homes.

Two in-depth group interviews constituted phase three of the research. These were carried out with Sally and Jean (whose details had been given to me by Holly, Kerry and Anna), and Chris, Kay and Angie (who contacted me almost a year after receiving one of my leaflets at the anti-CJB demonstration.) Again, these interviews were carried out in one of the women's homes.

All of these women were white and all clubbed and raved in and around London although many were not from this area originally. The women ranged from 19 to 35 years old and had a variety of different occupations. Several were students. Some were unemployed and some had temporary employment. Only two were involved in full-time and permanent paid work. All (except Michelle Pole about whom I have written elsewhere) have had their names changed.

All interviews took between one and four hours (depending upon how long the interviewee could spare). All were semi-structured and designed to leave conversation as open as possible. Interview questions were focused around the different women's clubbing and raving histories and around the significance of clubbing and raving within the broader contexts of their lives. When words like 'ecstatic', 'peak' or 'freedom' were used, I asked the women to clarify the meanings of such terms. And when they spoke about 'going mental' or 'losing it' for example, I asked them to be more specific about what they were getting at.

In general these questions were intended:

1) to get participants to speak about their personal histories of raving and clubbing and to indicate why such practices were important to them;
2) Building on (1), to get participants to make comparisons between different kinds of events. Often this led into discussion of identifications with *particular* kinds of musics, scenes and crowds;
3) To get participants to explain how they saw relations between men and women within contemporary dance cultures. This tended to lead into discussion about sexual pick-up; the significance of dress; the effects of drugs on sexual relations; the spatial organisation of bodies within events; feelings about safety and danger, and about what is considered 'appropriate' and 'inappropriate' behaviour;
4) To get women to talk in as much depth as possible about how they felt within different events. This included discussion of drug-experiences and dancing; interpersonal relations; physical and mental sensations; feelings of comfort and discomfort; the particular pleasures being sought within an event, and the potential 'obstacles' to these pleasures;
5) To elucidate the significance of clubbing within these women's lives. This led into discussion of commitments to work, family, lovers, children, and how these related to their involvements within rave. Similarly, talk about financial issues often arose and this commonly led into discussion of the lengths to which participants would go in order to attend an event;
6) Finally, to get individual women to say as much as they possibly could about what terms like 'freedom', 'self-expression' and 'liberation' (where these came up) meant to them.

The above is simply a list around which I tried to base interview conversation. It was, however, modified as the process went on and if something seemed to be emerging which I had not considered, this was built into my next interview plan. As I pointed out in the introductory chapter, my initial aim (which very much structured the focus of my first phase of interviewing including my MA research) was to make sense of the associations which raving women seemed to make between their dance cultural practices and notions about 'freedom'. In examining the data which emerged from this phase, these associations became clear. So too did an explicit and recurrent criticism of what were seen to be 'predatory' forms of masculinity, which the women tended to associate with pub and 'gig' scenes – and which the older women also associated with pre-rave nightclub cultures.

Within my second phase of interviews I therefore paid more attention to the criticisms of particular masculinities which appeared to emerge from phase one. Here, I wanted to explore in more detail precisely how what to me was a very clear 'semi-structure' of feminist feeling, as Angela McRobbie puts it, was being articulated. Although this did not really involve asking *different* questions of participants, it did involve probing some of their responses more forcefully, so that more was said about exactly how gender relations were seen to be played out within the rave event.

As I also pointed out within my introduction, I was at this time becoming increasingly aware of the fact that raving sometimes appeared to involve a certain degree of anxiety or fear for some of these interviewees. One interview at the start of my third phase, made this particularly clear. So phase three is structured around the same questions as were the previous two phases, but here, I also asked more about potential anxiety within an event. This involved questions about 'bad trips', 'negative vibes', 'aggressive' crowds, and about dance events which the women said that they did *not* enjoy.

Reading Data

All of the interviews were treated in terms of what can broadly be thought of as a thematic analysis, which involved identifying pertinent or recurrent themes from interviewee accounts, and considering these themes in relation to a broader cultural context. With these particular data and with my particular research questions in mind, this involved locating women's accounts in relation to a more general climate of sexual change. Where for example, a recurrent association is made between raving and being at 'home', this is examined in terms of why, at this point in time, the notion of 'belonging' might take the form that it does within these accounts. Likewise, where a form of resentment appears to emerge (as it frequently does) when these women imagine having to give up raving, this is considered in terms of shifting cultural discourses about female 'aging' and about femininity's traditional 'life-course'.

The data are, as I indicated earlier, drawn upon to address several different (although connected questions). It is examined in relation to questions about social and personal 'freedom', about the parallels between a popular post-feminism and new feminist figurations, and about the production of 'ecstatic' or 'peak' moments. Chapter 3 details the different ways in which rave and club cultures signify for, and are used by, the different interviewees. In outlining these individual actualisations of raving, the *just-barely-possible* connections between these participants are outlined. The major question around which the chapter is woven is: what does rave culture mean for these different women? What does this culture implicate in terms of wider issues around femininity, around aging and around contemporary senses of belonging for example?

Because I wanted to remain faithful to the specificities of given women's accounts however, the interviewees are introduced individually. An alternative would have been to group different subjects' accounts together under particular themes or discourses. I did not want to do this however and chose instead, to present these accounts as different and specific 'snap-shots'. This is a move towards retaining something of what Ernesto Laclau (1990) calls 'the dignity of the specific', and it is also a presentation which enables me to highlight themes which appeared particularly significant to an individual account. So Amy for example, talks a lot within our interview about her anxieties about getting old. It is something which very much marks her account. Other women however, also voiced similar anxieties (although these came to characterise their accounts less clearly). Presenting Amy's account as an individual one allows me to bring these other women into association with her, without overlooking their differences from her, and without suggesting that any two women are *the same*. Jane, on the other hand, tends to speak a lot about the 'freedom' she experiences within an event. Again, presenting her account as specific enables me to use it as a kind of skeleton upon which to lay similar aspects of other women's accounts. Teresa's account was characterised very much by her stress on the 'madness' she feels when raving. It is by no means an uncommon stress, but it seems to be very much the major thread of this particular account. Giving each interview a subtitle is an attempt at speaking in more than just interviewee names, a way of getting at more than just isolated, individual stories. As I argued earlier, my aim is neither to say what dance means *generally*, to women in *general*, nor to interpret the situations of isolated individual women. To reiterate, more general issues of the relations between rave and contemporary modes of femininity can only be addressed through the specifics of a given individual's actualisations of the possibilities inherent within a cultural situation. I have chosen to present the interview material as I have, because it enables me to work this way.

Chapter 3 is therefore about introducing all of these interviewees in terms of both their specificity and their associations with others. Chapter 4 looks to the resonances which these women's experiential accounts of rave culture have with Haraway's and Braidotti's work on feminist figurations. Here, I draw out recurrent themes from the data and explore these in terms of popular fictions of femininity. The aim is rather different from the one which structures Chapter 3 because here, I am more interested in thinking about these accounts collectively, and in terms of the ways in which subjectivity, femininity and the world are being storied within the accounts.

In Chapter 5, I concentrate on one interview in particular. This account is explored in terms of what it says about the work which goes into the production of an 'ecstatic' moment. Foucault's work on 'technologies of the self' provides a starting point for considering the various operations upon the self which can be involved in raving. I therefore focus primarily upon the one interview and highlight the various forces which are presented as 'disturbances' to a sought-after state, and the various ways in which such 'disturbances' are managed. This particular analysis problematises any oversimplistic association between raving and 'freedom'.

Of course and as should be obvious from my earlier discussions, my interpretation of interview material could have been done otherwise. I know that this material could have been drawn upon to say something quite different.

Ethnography and reflexivity

I have talked about the present study as one which is based primarily around the experiential accounts of female clubbers and ravers. But this was clearly not the only form of primary research which I conducted. Although I do not choose to call it 'participant observation', my research included extensive and ongoing involvement within nightclubs and raves. Although I did not operate within any kind of traditional ethnographic framework, I *was* at pains to visit as wide a variety of London-based dance events as possible. These included, free raves which were held in squatted buildings, disused warehouses or outdoors (and which were usually one-off events, publicised by fliers or word of mouth), all-women events, and a variety of techno-music events held in clubs. I therefore spent much time during my research, within clubs and raves, although I never felt comfortable, or particularly pushed towards, 'observing' in that detached way which the term 'participant observation' can imply. Because I was just as interested in experience and subjectivity as I was in things which could be seen or observed, I tended to concentrate, within these situations, upon what I was feeling, experiencing and thinking just as much as I focused on the outward behaviours of others. Of course these are extremely oversimplistic distinctions to make, but the point is that my aim was never really to take up the position of a detached onlooker.

My own experiences acted as 'data' and as a useful research resource in many different ways. For one thing, it acted as a background history and as a point of reference. But this was not simply a history of clubbing. Rather, it was a story about growing up. And perhaps the motivation behind the present study comes from my own inability to view raving as an isolated practice. For me, its significance stretched far beyond the physical practices of going to an event and dancing. But although I knew that in conducting this study, I was setting out to explore more than simply a social dance scene, precisely what might be involved was not entirely clear. For this reason, keeping a diary during this period very much served to clarify precisely what was tied up for me in the practices of rave. This was less a set of 'field notes' and more a 'personal' record of a 10-year period of living in 1990s London. It would be wrong to say that my own journey through this period somehow 'qualified' me to talk to, or *on behalf of* other women to whom raving had been an important part of this decade. But my own experiences did bring me close to many of the issues which participants went on to talk about within the interviews. At the same time, there were obviously many issues (such as those touched upon by the much younger women, and particularly by the two young single mothers) that were entirely outside my experiences at this time. And recognising these differences was important.

When I started my research then, I had already been a clubber for many years. I could never have experienced my situation as one of participatory, but nevertheless 'detached' observer. This was never my aim. I was already enmeshed in the culture I set out to do research on. Within sociology and anthropology alike, debate about participant observation has often focused upon the correct degree of involvement the observer should achieve. She must be neither too detached (in which case, 'insiders' may become suspicious), nor too involved (in which case she may find it difficult to 'get out', or difficult to sustain the level of critical distance necessary for study. She may also 'influence' the group in such a way as to raise questions about validity, bias and generalisability). These models and this language – which have now been thoroughly rethought within more contemporary and critical anthropology (Clifford, 1986) – imply clear distinctions between the world of the researcher, and that of the researched. The researcher temporarily enters the world of the researched, strategically assuming the part of a just-involved-enough observer. It is no surprise then, that the metaphor of the theatrical 'role' has traditionally been applied to the work of the ethnographer. Beneath this 'role' lies the more authentic, complete and real self, which is temporarily concealed in order to carry out observational research. Such ideas and language must, and indeed they are being, laid to rest. We need instead, to find a language to get at the connections between always-fragile, partial and never-complete situations. We can never entirely fill a situation – be this our 'own' or another's. We might however, touch, approximate or connect with another's located subjectivity. But this connection is faint, temporary and often just barely discernible.

The language of traditional ethnography is becoming less and less useful to our contemporary climate. The kind of approaches which focus upon a self-reflexive form of movement through different cultural contexts is, I believe, far more useful to a poststructuralist ethnographic practice. Grossberg for example, argues that the task of cultural criticism is to describe:

> vectors, distances and densities, intersections and interruptions, and
> the nomadic wandering (whether of people in everyday life or as

cultural critics) through this unequally and unstably organised field of tendential forces and struggles. (1988, p. 383)

This vision of a nomadic wandering is I believe, a more useful way of thinking about the work that we do as cultural critics. Grossberg pictures our work thus, as he writes of:

> ... the inevitability (and indeed the pleasurable and enabling possibilities) of different and temporary alliances, built upon different grounds, along different dimensions, with different intensities, as we move in different directions, without ever knowing precisely where we are going. (1988, p. 377)

Notes

1 See flier in previous chapter.
2 No distinction was made within these adverts between raves, 'free parties', and techno-music club-events. This is, I know important, and for some, it might be seen as a problem. My call however, was intentionally a general one to women involved in contemporary social dance scenes. Those who came forward often attended a combination of different kinds of events, although all identified themselves as 'ravers', defining a rave as usually an all-night techno-music event, at which the use of ecstasy and other drugs was normal.
3 See Pini and Terranova, 1996.

3
Moving Homes: Femininity under Reconstruction

> We are in the middle of an intrinsic change in the relations between men and women: a shift in power and values that is unravelling many of the assumptions not only of 200 years of industrial society, but also of millennia of traditions and beliefs. (Wilkinson, 1994, p. 1)

And so we reach the dance floor, since it is within the dance culture of clubs and raves that the new practices of the post-feminist and now post-AIDS generation are being publicly worked out. (Bradby, 1993, p. 165)

We are coming to believe that we are now living through a moment of quite radical sexual-political change. Traditional values, beliefs and expectations are shifting. What it means to do masculinity and femininity has altered. We have entered the era of so-called 'post-feminism'.

In her recent work on new girls' magazines, Angela McRobbie examines one manifestation of emerging modes of femininity as she outlines the extent to which femininity has been freed from its traditional associations with passivity, sexual modesty and 'innocence'. In the magazines which McRobbie examines, young heterosexual women are addressed as part of a sexually desiring and lustful audience, keen for both sexual adventure and for the opportunities to partake of practices which were once the primary preserve of men. Boozing, partying and 'shagging' girls have thus moved to the fore of our cultural landscape. Something has clearly changed, suggests McRobbie, when questions about the quality of the orgasm have replaced the concerns with getting and keeping a man which characterised girls' magazines of the past. She argues then:

> What I have called 'new sexualities' is possibly the most visible evidence of the changing world of magazines. These are images and texts which break decisively with the conventions of feminine behaviour by representing girls as crudely lustful, desiring young women. For this new kind of (typically heterosexual) girl, frank information, advice and knowledge about sex is a prerequisite for her adventures as a 'serial dater' (*Just Seventeen*). And so the first task to consider here is what is going on when oral sex and the quality of the orgasm are the cover stories in magazines read by girls as young as 13 years old. (1997c, pp. 195–6)

It is not only within the culture of new girls' magazines that we find the emergence of the 'feisty', 'snogging', and boozing young woman who parties as hard and as often as her male counterpart, and who embodies sexual attitudes traditionally associated with masculinity. The female figures who appeared on programmes such as *The Girlie Show*, *God's Gift* and *Pyjama Party* (irrespective of how popular or unpopular these might have been) constituted televisual representations of the so-called 'babe' who poses in a style previously associated with passivity and sexual invite but who restates this look in terms of an assertiveness and a crude (or what might once have been considered 'vulgar') sexual desire.

Alongside these new media representations of sexually demanding and desiring heterosexual women, statistics indicate that more and more women are openly asserting their preference for one-night-stands over monogamous, long-term relations. A no-commitment attitude to hetero-sex and a refusal (for the present anyway) to 'settle down' in a relationship, is becoming a much more common feature of contemporary fictions of femininity. Furthermore, the recent appearance within popular literature of images of independent, drug-taking female clubbers indicates one version of the popular 'post-feminist' who parties, has sex and 'mouths off' without the constraints traditionally placed upon her to stay sober, respectable and to 'find a man'. The female figures presented within Geraldine Geraghty's *Raise Your Hands* (1996) and Irvine Walsh's *Ecstasy* (1996) have, for example, become familiar characters within a contemporary cultural context. 'Pilled-up' party girls no longer appear strange, vulgar or pathological. Femininity thus appears to be undergoing some kind of potentially quite radical transformation. Although no one is suggesting that such a transformation is happening evenly or uniformly across the social spectrum, there *is* a general acceptance that we are currently witnessing the emergence of new ways of being women-in-culture. Barbara Bradby suggests that the social dance floor constitutes one space wherein such new ways of being are publicly worked out, and what I want to do in this chapter is explore what women's experiential accounts of their club and rave practices tell us about not only the transformations which femininity is now undergoing, but also about the difficulties of living through these changes, and of negotiating the contradictions which these throw up. To reiterate a point I made in my introductory chapter, the stories which follow are stories about raving but they speak of so much more than simply what goes on within any rave event. What look simply like stories about a dance-music culture are in fact far more complex, and implicate far more issues than we might immediately imagine. The questions asked of these data then, are not simply about what goes on within any given rave event. Instead, I want to draw attention to what these accounts tell us about how femininity is now articulated and embodied. What do the accounts say about emerging modes of femininity; about shifts in female experiences of aging? What role do raving and club-bing play in relation to such shifts? And what *are* the new concerns, anxieties, practices and desires of what Bradby calls a 'post-feminist' generation, or what McRobbie refers to as a generation marked by a 'semi-structure' of feminist feeling? As she puts it:

> But what I am referring to here is the deeper change in conscious-ness which has affected the outlook, values and expectations of women and young women, from different social backgrounds, from different parts of the country, from different cultures. It is difficult to generalise across such a large sector of the population. It is not as though women share anything like a single set of values or beliefs. Nor has change affected women homogenously. By exploring the climate of change in the culture of young women today one is tapping into something which exists in a state of disaggregated latency, a 'semi-structure of feeling' to re-phrase

Raymond Williams, which surfaces at unexpected moments in
unexpected ways. (1997b, p. 159)

Is a new type of 'feminism' evident within the accounts of raving
women, and if so, what does this look like? If, raving is experienced
as enabling a passage into some kind of 'elsewhere', then what is
this, and what goes on here? What is this 'other' and what different
articulations of subjectivity are seen to emerge here. These are some
of the questions around which the present and the following chapter
are structured. In this chapter, I want to indicate what raving means
to the different women who were interviewed. I want to focus upon
what role this plays within their lives and in particular, I want to
highlight the alternative senses of self which many claim to experience within the rave event. In the following chapter, I shall build
upon this and consider what such 'alternatives' might say about
emerging forms of femininity more generally.

As I indicated in the introduction to Part II, I introduce all of the
interviews individually, and in so doing, I weave together a collage
of 'snapshots' of particular negotiations of being as a contemporary
female raver. Although I am attempting to present each interviewee
(or group of interviewees) in such a way as to hold onto the specificity of her/their stories, I also want to trace the connections between
different interviewees, themes and stories. A given interviewee is
not therefore presented or discussed in terms of a discreet or self-
contained 'block'. Instead, I have opted to isolate a particular theme
which seemed to emerge from a given interview in a particularly
clear way. I have therefore given a subtitle to each interview. This is
intended simply as a way of opening up from a particular woman's
account a theme which is then supported or touched upon within
other women's accounts. It is also a way of presenting these data in a
more 'conversational' way, which respects both the dignity of the
specific and the potential for the just-barely-possible connections of
which I spoke in the previous chapter. However, not all of the interviewees are discussed in equal depth. Michelle in particular (because
she was interviewed as part of a project about different 'Freedom to
Party' movements and because the interview dealt less directly with
questions about women's experiences of rave and more with issues
concerning attempts at legislative intervention into Britain's dance
scenes) is discussed more briefly. Sally and Jean (because Chapter 5

deals in such depth with their accounts in particular) are discussed here only where they add weight to other women's accounts. And as I explained earlier, Catherine, Miriam, Ann and Elaine (because these women were interviewed for a much earlier project on women and the early British rave scene) are not discussed separately, but are instead, referenced where relevant.

Clearly, the themes which I have chosen to isolate do not say *everything* that could be said about any given account. The practices of raving and clubbing clearly play different roles within different women's lives. These are situated practices, and the conditions of their situations are all particular. I have tried to remain faithful to such differences, although I am more interested in the interconnections between these accounts. These emerge gradually as the chapter builds up. The motivation behind this choice of presentation comes, therefore, from my reluctance to disembody and classify different interviewees (which, as I suggested previously would, I believe, have been the result had I chosen to collapse different stories into something I might have called 'themes' or 'discourses'). Alternatively, I could have written about the particular practices and understandings of different women, as though these spoke about nothing more than the experiences of unique individuals. This would hardly have constituted a cultural study. The story woven in what follows, highlights generals by attending to specifics.

Amy: saddies, aging and finding home

> I'm really sorry I found it so late. It's a scene where I just really feel quite at home. This is the first time that I really felt this is what I wanted from clubs. (Amy)

Amy is a 32-year-old woman who originally comes from Kent, but now lives in London where she is doing temporary office work. She explains that as a teenager, she did not go clubbing very often because it was usually difficult for her to get home after an event, and also because she did not enjoy the 'beer-boy element' which she says characterised club cultures at the time. Although when she was in her twenties, she would club occasionally (about once every two months), Amy says that she has only been a 'proper clubber or raver for the past four years'. Many of Amy's close friends no longer rave with her, either because they have become bored by the scene, or because they have suffered negative effects from the frequent or long-term use of ecstasy. These effects include depression and anxiety attacks. Amy herself, takes 'E' and Speed every time she raves (which is now usually at least once a week), although on several occasions during our interview, she indicates that she regularly worries about the long-term effects that this might be having upon her health. (And I shall say more about the significance of recreational drug-use later). Despite such worries however, Amy tells me that if she imagines one day looking back upon this stage of her life, raving will be remembered as providing 'the best times of an otherwise quite miserable period'. When asked to elaborate upon this, she says:

> I feel quite down about other things that are going on in my life. I don't like the work I'm doing. It's sort of . . . well, it's temporary and it's not fulfilling. I'm not really in a relationship – not that I really *want* to be, but there's just nothing there really. I'm just not really where I want to be in my life at the moment. But clubbing is a place where . . . um, I just get so very much out of it and being part of it and it's where I can feel that I really am part of something.

One of the most striking and consistent features to emerge from this interview (although it is by no means uncommon) is the association which Amy makes between raving and 'being at home', and this is what I want to concentrate upon for the present. In particular – and because the account raises such interesting questions about belonging and aging – I want to consider what it says about changing fictions of 'adult' femininity, and changing senses of female belongingness. To return to a statement cited earlier, Amy explains: 'When I discovered rave, I just finally found a place that felt like home. Like being in the bosom of my family.'

Later in the interview Amy describes a 'pop disco event' which she recently attended, but did *not* enjoy, in similar terms: 'I had a less good time and it made me feel more distanced and it made me feel less . . . feel less like I was at home.'

Throughout the interview, the rave environment is consistently constructed as one which offers Amy an enormous sense of comfort and belonging. It is 'home' and 'the bosom of her family'. Significantly, this image stands in stark contrast to a 'lack of fit' which Amy describes experiencing within other spheres of her life – and particularly within her work place and within her sexual relationships with men. She does not really belong within her work place – because she feels that she has been labelled a 'right-on' feminist and therefore does not fit into what is a largely male environment. As she puts it:

> I'm probably quite aggressively 'right-on'. I mean I started work recently and it's quite male and quite um … There's lots of sort of wise-cracks all the time. I really got myself labelled. I mean, I'd hardly been there a week when they kind of labelled me as this kind of politically correct feminist – in a *very* strong way.

And in reflecting upon her current situation as a single woman, Amy suggests an equal lack of fit when it comes to sexual relationships:

> I suppose I'm not in one – a steady sexual relationship – now, because … well, maybe it's … I mean that I just didn't really fit that properly. It wasn't really me. And I don't really plan to do that again now – not for the moment, but I'm sure I will.

A contrast between the sense of belonging provided by the social dance-floor and the sense of alienation which Amy suggests in discussing work and relationships, is consistent throughout the account. Indeed, the rave environment is repeatedly constructed as filling some kind of gap within her life. Amy is not where she wants to be in her life more generally. She is down and unfulfilled. The rave event provides her with the 'best times' of this 'otherwise quite miserable period'. It is 'home' and like 'the bosom of her family'.

The theme of belonging which emerges from Amy's account very clearly adds weight to Barbara Bradby's observation that the rave environment is commonly understood and experienced as providing some kind of 'antidote' to a general sense of alienation from society, which today's young people often experience. Bradby argues this in referencing several young British ravers to whom the 'enfolding, warm sense of community' which they find within the rave, stands in stark contrast not only to a general sense of British despair but also to the macho and sexist attitudes which are seen to characterise other music scenes. Like these young people, Amy consistently constructs the rave environment as a warm, welcoming and comforting pocket, within a wider, colder and more alienating world. But, her account (like many of the others which I shall discuss) arguably suggests something *more* than this, or something more specific about this alienation. It strikes me that – in one important respect at least – Amy is perhaps touching on more than just a *general* alienation from society. It is not simply the world of work and romance, or even something very general called 'society' which Amy appears to be suggesting an alienation from. Rather, what the account seems to suggest is a much more *specific* alienation from what we might call the traditional 'landmarks' of femininity. And this is something which emerges time and again throughout these data; a sense that a growing fluidity, confusion or ambiguity is coming to surround femininity. In Amy's case, this sense of uncertainty seems most obvious when she thinks about her status as an 'adult'. Her practices as a raver clearly clash with accepted and recognisable definitions of 'adult' femininity. And, like many of the other interviewees, as she reflects upon her practices, Amy repeatedly questions herself. How, as a grown woman, can she have such attachments to rave? How is she to reconcile such attachments with her status as an adult? Do such attachments make her somehow 'immature'? Is there something wrong with her? She says:

> You know, I guess it is really a little...well, I don't know. I do really enjoy this but perhaps I am being a bit...maybe, I am too old for this but it feels right, so I don't know. I suppose it's not really what you think of when you think of a 32 year old but for now, it does feel right for me.

Amy thus suggests a certain lack of fit in relation to her ideas about being an 'adult' woman. She appears both anxious and confused about getting older. Is she, she repeatedly asks herself, too old to be clubbing and raving? The thought that she may have to stop raving, because this might be an 'inappropriate' practice for a woman of her age to be engaged in causes her sadness. In terms of tradition, it seems 'inappropriate', yet still 'it feels right'. More than this, it is actually one of the most important things in her life at the moment. A contradiction is thus evident between ideas about 'appropriate' adult femininity, and Amy's desires to rave. She may, she fears, soon start looking like what she calls a 'saddie'. As she puts it:

You know I'm worried that . . . You know, I'm 32 now so I'm old to go to clubs – many people think. Although sometimes I go to clubs where there *are* a few older people, but the club that I go to at the moment, that I really, really like on Friday night, is quite young. I don't feel uncomfortable *there* because I'm not the *only* one and also it *is* quite un-judgemental as I said. There's something quite generous about the whole ecstasy-culture which means 'good on ya, 'cause you're into this scene' and it doesn't matter whether you're older or whatever. Um, but that runs out, I'm sure. You still unfortunately look like a sad-case if you're . . . well, the fact that in a while, I'll probably think 'no, I'm a saddie now' or *other people* will think I'm a saddie – I'm not worried enough about that now and I'll just brazen it out – does mean that whole attitude, and I'll have to give it up and that makes me feel really sad, and that makes me sorry in a sense that I didn't start earlier.

When I ask Amy to say more about her sadness, she explains:

You know, I just really find it . . . it's a really wonderful thing for me to be part of now, because like I say, there really isn't much else. I know I maybe will have to stop but I don't want to and it makes me sad – very sad really.

Andrew Ross has argued that the social dance floor has long provided a kind of 'safe haven' for socially marginalised groups (1994, p. 10). I want to suggest that Amy, like many of these interviewees, appears to indicate that the dance floor can become precisely such a space for women who now feel marginalised by traditional fictions of femininity and traditional stories about femininity's 'rightful' place and life course. Of course, this is not *all* that the rave environment can signify and it would be wrong to state the point too strongly. These data do however, suggest a connection for some women, between the 'world' of rave and an ambiguity now surrounding ideas about femininity and 'adulthood' and an uncertainty surrounding the question of 'what next?'

Like Amy, Teresa is worried that her clubbing practices may well not fit with her situation as an 'adult' woman. Is her behaviour, she asks herself, 'appropriate' for a woman of 26? How does it fit with her ideas about what being a 'grown up' woman are all about? In response to my very general question about the appeal which rave holds for her, she talks about having found a place within the rave environment where she can be 'completely at one with [her] self'. Still, she has worries that this might be 'inappropriate' for a woman of her age. As she puts it:

Sometimes I think well, maybe I'm too old for this. Maybe I shouldn't be here. Maybe it's *not* right. Not 'cause I don't *want* to be here, but is it ... am I getting too old for this thing? I don't *feel* too old for this thing. Or is this thing too young for me, you know? See I always used to think next year I'm going to grow up and I'm not going to be wanting to do these things. But I don't know 'cause it hasn't happened. Maybe one day I'll wake up and think no, I don't want that any more. But I just can't properly imagine it though.

Both Teresa and Amy thus suggest something about an erosion of the traditional markers of 'adult' femininity. Recognisable signs of a transition from a clearly delineated 'youth', to a clearly delineated 'adulthood', no longer seem to make much sense to such women. What next, when marriage, motherhood or even a clear career-path do not hail so forcefully or successfully? Like Amy, Teresa is single (describing herself as having been moving between 'temporary and casual relationships for the past six years'). And like Amy, she is doing a number of part-time, temporary jobs although she is also studying on a degree course. Many aspects of these women's lives simply fail to accord with conventional ideas about adult femininity. They are not girlfriends, not wives and not mothers, but neither are they the 'career women' we often hear of as the alternative to these.

I have written elsewhere about how women in the past have tended to give up social dancing once they became married (Pini, 1996.) Marriage commonly signalled a next developmental 'stage' for heterosexual women. For many women today however, such clear markers of a 'next stage', have largely disappeared. What does adult femininity today entail? How do I know when I have reached it? By what cultural markers am I to gauge it? Amy, like Teresa seems to be left unsure about how to situate herself in relation to her idea of the adult woman. Maybe 'next year' Teresa will 'grow up'. At the moment, she cannot imagine it though. Perhaps, 'in a while' Amy will think 'no'. For now, the women remain unclear. And centrally, this uncertainty is about not being able to properly imagine a 'next stage' – an 'adult' situation.

Although Bradby reads the particular articulations of femininity emerging within contemporary club cultures as signalling a general 'prolongation of youth', it is perhaps more accurate and useful to view these as indicators of the emergence of new modes of *adult* femininity. Such modes of being may indeed appear 'juvenile' when measured against our traditional markers of 'adult' femininity, but the fact is that many women who are well into their twenties and thirties are having to face 'adult' responsibilities (including child-rearing and earning a wage), whilst simultaneously facing the ambiguities and confusion surrounding precisely how adult femininity is to be 'done' – embodied, recognised and articulated – within a contemporary context.

The kinds of questions which both Amy and Teresa ask themselves as they reflect upon their practices, are raised by many of the other interviewees as well. The regularity of such questions suggests that something more than simply a failure or reluctance on the part of women to 'grow up', is going on. This appears to be about much more than an evasion of adulthood and responsibility. Rather, the signifiers or markers of 'grown-up' femininity have simply become less recognisable. What happens when marriage, motherhood, and a recognisable form of 'settlement' seem unlikely in the near future? And when at the same time, the opportunities *are* opening for more and more women to club, take drugs and stay out dancing all night? Refiguring 'adulthood' in relation to such a shifting situation is clearly confusing. And this confusion speaks again and again through these women's accounts.

Significantly, as this confusion or breakdown of certainty comes to mark heterosexual femininity, the rave environment comes to be viewed by women like these interviewees, as a kind of 'home'. But, if this environment is constructed as a 'homely' one, then this is a rather different image of 'home' from the one usually conjured up by the term. We may indeed still be talking about a sense of comfort and belonging, but we are no longer talking about fixity, stability or familiarity here. Instead, Amy (like many of the other women) paints a picture of home as one in which she can go 'mad', be 'confused', and generally 'lose it' in ways which she otherwise cannot. This home is temporary and – it seems – all the more intense and pleasurable, precisely because of its temporary or fleeting nature. The sense of pleasurable or ecstatic confusion which Amy describes is consistent across this sample. And finding a 'home' within madness and confusion is touched upon within almost all of these accounts. Indeed, club organiser and DJ Louise tells me that most of the people she plays for at an event 'are there in the first place to go psychotic'. This, she says is the whole point. Amy herself says: 'I just let go. Half the time I don't . . . I'm not sure *what's* going on, and that I think is the greatest sensation. I really do love that. Teresa makes a very similar point:

> You don't know exactly *what* it is that's happening to you sometimes. You think, oh my God, is that a sex sensation, or a peace sensation? Is it a love sensation or a panic sensation? Is it mellow, or 'rushy'? I don't know. There's a tingling going on *somewhere*. It's like shit, what *is* this? But I don't know *what* it is.

As will become clear, Amy and Teresa's stress upon the pleasures of 'madness' and 'confusion' which raving is seen to involve, is a very familiar one. So too is a construction of the rave event as a kind of 'home'. Why then, if 'home' has become filled with a sense of confusion and uncertainty, should it be considered so appealing by these women?

Barbara O'Connor (in Thomas (1997)) has argued in relation to recreational dance (although she focuses specifically on set-dancing) that regular participation within social dance groups can come to play a fundamental role in the construction of new communities, or what (drawing upon Scott Lash) she calls new 'communitas'. With the erosion of traditional communities, the disintegration of both religious institutions and the nuclear family, and within a context where marriage is increasingly becoming what McRobbie (1994) calls 'a temporary contract', *new* communities, *new* senses of affective identity and *new* types of what Lash calls 'sociations' emerge. One thing which the present data perhaps suggest is that at a time when women are becoming increasingly alienated from ideas about their 'appropriate' life-course, the social dance-floor can indeed become a space which promises an immediate sense of belongingness, or what

O'Connor describes as an instant and ephemeral community. It can become a new kind of 'home'. Almost all of these women stress for instance, how 'in touch' with music, with the 'spiritual' and with others they can be within an event. It is a language of comfort and belongingness. At the same time however, many emphasise and celebrate the autoeroticism, narcissism, 'madness' and self-absorption involved in raving. If rave culture constitutes some kind of 'community' for these women, then this is a community in which both collectivity and individuality, belonging and anonymity, feeling 'whole' and feeling 'dispersed' are made possible. It is a community where both 'mad' confusion and a sense of absolute 'oneness' can be simultaneously articulated. In so many respects, these accounts suggest the kinds of magical resolution of wider contradictions which Dick Hebdige (1979) among others have written about in relation to youth subcultures. Contradictions and tensions are expressed within these subcultures, and somehow 'magically resolved' at the level of signs. Although I do not think that it is particularly useful to view contemporary dance cultures as 'subcultures', and although many of the present interviewees are not really 'youths', much of what these women say does suggest some kind of resolution taking place within the rave event. Here, a certain 'autonomy' and self-centredness can coexist with a sense of being involved within the generation of a bigger community and a wider bonding or unification.

As I pointed out earlier, Bradby touches upon the collective and unifying discourses generated within rave culture, as she describes how the young people she references view rave as providing a warm and enfolding antidote to the alienation of wider British society. I have suggested however, that for the present interviewees, this appears to be about more than simply finding solutions to a *general* sense of alienation from broader society. A more specific alienation is, I believe, being referenced here. What many of the women appear to be talking about is a distance from conventional fictions of femininity including fictions about its 'adult' form. The traditional markers by which female maturation has been gauged, have become less and less clear and this is obvious from the data. The landmarks of femininity are collapsing. Teresa for example, claims that she will *know* that she is an 'adult' when her desire to rave ends. Perhaps she will wake one day to find that she is an adult because this desire has passed. Still, she cannot really imagine this. For now, the thought of what her own embodiment of an adult femininity will feel or look like remains rather vague. This is a self-sufficient, independent woman in her mid-twenties. Yet, she cannot recognise herself as an 'adult'. Being an 'adult' is for many of these women (including Clare, Anna, Kerry, Holly and Jane) very much associated with being more 'sane' or less confused than they presently feel themselves to be. But rather than viewing such women as somehow 'immature', it is I believe, more accurate to see them as embodying a wider cultural 'troubling' of femininity. The fact that so many of the present interviewees speak of just not knowing how to recognise themselves as 'proper' adults and just not knowing how to situate themselves in relation to a broader 'life-course' suggests that confusion has perhaps become an integral part of the reconstructions which femininity is currently undergoing.

It could of course be argued that Amy and Teresa's anxieties about their age simply speak of a more general cultural fetishisation of 'youth' – about their situation within a context wherein 'youth' becomes, as Simon Reynolds has argued, almost the very definition of the healthy body (1989). But the situation is far more complex. When asked directly, neither Amy nor Teresa say that they mind getting older, nor the *idea* of getting older. Indeed, both claim to be actually looking forward to finding out precisely what they will do or want next. Thirty-one-year-old Clare articulates this sense of looking forward to the as-yet unknown in particularly clear terms:

> It'll be nice to find something different to take up so much energy and . . . and just something that I involve myself in so much. I mean if I *did* find something else . . . plus it would be cheaper and healthier. I *do* see myself kind of getting out of this scene and wanting something else. But I don't see what it is right now.

Like Teresa, Clare is faced, it seems, *not* with problems about actually doing adult (taken to broadly mean responsible, independent and self-sufficient) femininity as a practice, but rather, with problems about actually imagining how to embody and articulate this in relation to its traditional signifiers. To reiterate, contemporary modes of adult femininity are still very much under reconstruction and women such as these ones speak as though they are living through the dust thrown up by if not a demolition, then a quite rapid disintegration of established ideas. And many seem unable – for now at least – to imagine beyond this haze.

The failure to imagine 'beyond' raving (which as a practice is in many ways associated with not being a 'proper' adult woman) is a consistent one among the 'older' women in this sample. Teresa says for example:

> If I had to stop that, I don't know *what* I would do. I don't think I could handle not doing it. But what would I do instead? After that, what *is* there? There must be something, but what *is* it?

What such claims would seem to indicate is the inadequacy of a traditional developmental model in relation to a contemporary landscape of femininity. Such tradition no longer makes sense. The idea of movement from 'enclosure' within a familial home to 'enclosure' within a marital home, upon which such a model rests, can no longer be a taken-for-granted. Such routes are breaking down. And for some of the present interviewees, rave can it seems, come to fill the gap left by the breakdown of these traditional fictions, and it *can* come to provide a space and sense of 'mad' belonging for women to whom these fictions no longer make sense or carry any promise, or even any meaningful fantasy of coherence. In such cases rave culture seems to offer a sense of belongingness where a suturing into more traditional stories of femininity is no longer so effective.

Amy casts rave as 'other' to both marriage and motherhood – things which she does not plan for her near future, but things which are clearly seen as signals of the end of her raving days. Like many of these interviewees, Amy imagines that marriage and motherhood should or will provide some kind of 'next stage' in her life. But – and again, this is a common feature throughout these data – 'marriage' and 'becoming a mother' appear as almost 'fantasmatic signifiers' of a form of more stable and settled future which is yet-to-come and the *desire* for which is also yet-to-come. These are not yet here. Amy for example, says:

> I do think of it [raving] as something I'll have to stop at some point. But not because I plan to get married or have children or anything. So far, I don't plan to do either of those things, but

I suppose *that's* when I'll know – when I'm settled or having a child or something.

Clare, who *is* in a 'steady' heterosexual relationship similarly evokes the image of the 'settled mother' to imagine beyond her current identification with rave. Again however, she appears unclear and uncertain. It is not simply *becoming* a 'settled mother', but more the *desire* to become one that she appears to be talking about and expecting:

If we decided to have children, I'd probably stop. If we *do*, but we don't plan to. I'm sure I'll want that maybe. It hasn't happened so far but it could and then, I won't carry on. Well, I won't be able to do this and I probably won't *want* to do this.

Later, Clare says of her relationship with her partner:

Settling down is what ... Yeah, it's what I thought I always wanted, but it's not. No, it *is* right for me, but it's not enough. It's not everything and sometimes I think it ought to be – and so does he think this.

These women may well express a desire for some 'next stage' clarity, but it seems that traditional organisations of 'settlement' – as these are structured around marriage and motherhood, no longer work so effectively. Even Sally and Jean (who *are* mothers) say that they had believed that upon having become pregnant, their desire to rave would have subsided. Instead, just two or three months after having had their children, the women had returned to raving on a regular basis. Jean says:

That was it right, no more. No more doing that when you're pregnant and you know, it's not right, Nah. That's what I *thought* right. But nah, didn't last. I didn't hold it up 'cause you know, I'm back there in the clubs and it was good you know.

To reiterate, for many of these women at least, an uncertainty seems to surround ideas about how femininity and adult femininity are now to be done. A certain confusion is obvious. In certain respects, raving seems to provide one way of both playing out this 'confusion' and of posing it as a new norm. In constituting a scene whose central raison d'être is in many ways about 'going mental', 'losing it' and getting 'out of it' ('it's about going psychotic', Louise tells me), rave makes for a communal expression of, and a collective being within, 'uncertainty'.

Of course, men too may enjoy the sense of 'madness' which can be generated within the rave environment. What is significant for the present study however, is what stories like Amy's and Teresa's say about how femininity is changing. Here are women who identify far more closely with stories about belonging within the 'mad' world opened up within the rave event, than they do with more traditional fictions of female belonging. And these are not teenagers. Amy is 32 and Teresa is 26. Their attachments to the world of clubs and raves is – in traditional terms – unusual for women of their age. Neither woman can really imagine beyond raving. Neither is really sure what might be 'next'. And neither really wants to let go of her identification with rave. Women like Amy and Teresa are actually engaged in, and attached to, practices which in the past have been more closely associated with masculinity or with adolescence. That such practices are now being openly embraced by women of their age, indicates the extent to which adult femininity has been wrenched from its traditional associations with enclosure and settlement.

It is I think, very significant that the playing out of a kind of 'madness' which these women speak of, *is* a communal enactment – a collective and ecstatic staging of ambiguity and 'madness', which simultaneously allows for the generation of a shared sense of belongingness and of community. In many respects, rave seems to draw these aspects of belongingness and community out of confusion and ambiguity, appearing to provide some kind of both symbolic and practical solution. Amy for example, when asked to say more about what her rave 'home' offers her that she does not find within other spheres of her life, concentrates upon how it enables strangers to bond so quickly, and how she manages to find a sense of 'calm' and 'comfort' within the 'madness' of an event:

> I like . . . like I said, I like the fact that I can merge into somewhere strange with people I don't really know and get so close and be so calm and comfortable within a crowd which is all losing it together. That's a major aspect of it.

Catherine says something similar:

> It's just the absolute feeling of belonging and love you get
> and ... and just getting 'out of it' with everyone else. It's mad but
> it's safe. Kind of you don't sort of ... you can 'lose it' but everyone
> else is *too*. So it's different. It wouldn't be the same if you didn't
> have *everyone* dancing and *everyone* pilled-up and *everyone* together
> in the lights and dancing. It's ... that's really important – having
> the crowd do it together and go mental.

Jane, whose account I shall move to next, also focuses upon this perceived coming together within rave of the 'private' and the 'public', the
self and the other, as she compares the dance floor with the bedroom:

> It's almost like dancing in your own bedroom, only with a bit of
> added impetus because there's hundreds of other people there.
> It's ... No, it's more than just a bit of added impetus. It's really
> important. You feel like it's your own private space and also a
> more public space. Like you're doing something more personal
> with hundreds of other people and getting really close to those
> hundreds of other people.

Jane: freedom, me and self-expression

Jane is a 28-year-old woman from East London. Although at the time
of interview, Jane was clubbing less often than she had been up until
a year beforehand, she still attends raves and clubs at least once a
month and she still very much identifies herself as a 'raver'. Jane no
longer uses drugs when raving, primarily because she worries about
the effects that this might have on her health. She has only stopped
using dance drugs over the past year however.

Although it is by no means unusual, one of the most obvious
themes to emerge from Jane's account, is an association between raving, self-expression and 'freedom'. For Jane, this 'freedom' is partly
about a release from her part-time job as a counsellor. Given the
nature of her work, it is perhaps not surprising that Jane puts such
stress upon the *self*-pleasure which raves afford her, although this is
a common emphasis throughout the data. For Jane, raving is very
much about letting go of the 'conformity' and responsibility she
associates with her day-to-day life and work:

If say, one of my clients saw me when I was clubbing, or some-body who was from a professional day-world came and saw me clubbing, it would *not* be ideal. It's like oh no, I *don't* want that to happen. It's about letting go of being conformist, and being professional and proper and together. It's other to presenting that face of you. It's not necessarily the dark side of you. But it's the messy side of you.

Jane's emphasis upon *self*-expression and *self*-pleasure is reinforced as she repeatedly speaks of the 'autoerotic' sensations which she experiences on the rave dance floor. She explains, for example:

When I go raving it's very um . . . well, one word that really comes to mind is autoerotic. Because you're getting off on yourself. And you can dance quite sexily and you can enjoy it and you can get really into being a sexual being. It can be sexual, but it's a kind of self-contained sexual, so that autoerotic spreads out – out of the erotic and into a whole personality thing. It's something about you're fulfilling yourself. There's something about a rave club which is in essence 'auto' and the autoerotic comes into it. The auto . . . I don't know what other phrase you could put together with it but 'self'.

The theme of autoeroticism or *self*-pleasure also comes up in many of the other interviews and almost all of the women speak of sexual pleasures focused on the 'self' or of feeling sensuous about their own bodies when dancing (and I shall come back to this in the following chapter). Amy for example, uses the term narcissistic:

It's more getting to be a solitary thing, like taking pleasure in your own body in a way that's . . . it's quite separate from anything else. It's quite narcissistic and self-absorbed.

And Holly explains:

You *do* feel sexual on 'E' but it's more kind of contained within yourself rather than you want to express it to somebody else.

Jane contrasts the autoerotic and *self*-focused pleasures of raving with ideas about being an object in someone *else's* eyes:

> But if somebody comes up and starts dancing with you, it's not always ideal because *then* you've got to be erotic in somebody *else's* eyes and then you become a performance, whereas before you've been performing to yourself. But as soon as you perform to somebody else, it changes it.

An emphasis upon *self*-pleasure is thus common across this sample of women as a whole, although and as I have already pointed out, this sits alongside an equal emphasis on the senses of collectivity, unity and connectedness generated within the rave environment, and the feeling of belonging within 'something bigger' which this affords. This apparently contradictory stress is clearly summed up by Clare, who explains:

> You *do* really feel connected, but...you *do* feel part of a bigger community, but you also feel like you're very much focused on yourself too. I'm not sure. I don't know how to put it really. It's like you feel both bounded in yourself and part of something where everyone is intact too. Maybe it's because you know that everyone's sort of feeling the same way and somehow that makes...it means that you're connected in knowing you're on the same wave-length.

I suggested earlier that for some of these interviewees, the rave appears to offer the possibilities for a public playing out of a kind of ambiguity or confusion. This sense of fluidity or uncertainty is further reinforced when the women speak about 'sexual', 'sensual' or 'erotic' sensations within a rave event. Many say that they simply cannot put these sensations into words. They do not know what to call these or how to interpret them. Statements like 'It's not sexual but orgasmic' (Miriam) 'Well, it's sexual but it isn't.' (Clare) or 'It's sexual in a different way' (Chris) are common and I shall return to this in the following chapter.

I have also argued that in one sense, the rave space is perhaps so highly valorised by these women because it affords some sense of belonging within a wider context where notions of female belonging are becoming more and more blurred. But, this is not *simply* a sense of belonging within something 'bigger' (such as the 'community' made up of a rave crowd for instance). It is also about a sense of 'belonging' within *oneself*. Jane's stress on the self-centredness, or self-focusedness which she feels when raving, is echoed throughout almost all of the other interviewee accounts. Many of the women thus appear to be describing a process of 'finding' themselves through 'loss'; through losing themselves to something 'bigger'. Jane, for instance, says:

> Although you're aware of yourself, you're in something bigger than yourself. And you can just spread out and your boundaries are just so stretched out, it isn't *you* any more. It's a whole thing.

And Catherine and Amy, whilst stressing the extent to which rave is about the 'freedom' to *really be yourself*, simultaneously, speak of *losing* the self:

> It's like being part of one big coordinated animal that just moves, and you're part of it. And it doesn't really matter if you personally stop, because even if you just stand there, it carries on and you feel you are still part of it. (Catherine)

> It's really like you have spread out of your own individual boundaries, and you lose your limits. You feel like you really are bigger or part of something bigger. (Amy)

Helen Wilkinson argues in her study of 'Generations and the Genderquake' that contemporary modes of femininity are coming to be characterised by an apparent contradiction (1994). On the one hand, she claims, today's young women appear to valorise independence and autonomy, whilst on the other, expressing a need for some kind of community-belongingness and what she calls 'spiritual wholeness'. The accounts of the present interviewees certainly suggest such a contradiction. And, in many respects, the rave space is seen to somehow resolve this tension. As a space which encourages the development of both a 'friendly' and 'egalitarian' sense of community (although this is of course, a rather problematic fiction to buy into) and of an absolute sense of self-absorption it encourages the development of a sense of 'oneness' with both crowd and self.

Significantly, if the rave environment is seen by these women to provide a 'comfortable' space for the playing out of a sense of 'belonging' and 'madness', then (and again, this is stressed by almost all of the interviewees) this is also centrally because it is seen to involve new forms of *masculinity*. To return to a statement by Jane which I cited earlier:

> Before rave, it was the worst thing possible. Lots of pissed men and a really lairy letchy space where you couldn't do anything without being interfered with. There were loads of pissed blokes and kind of out for the fucking lay. And out with loads of other blokes as well. That kind of scenario. Blokes trying to impress their mates and thinking they can chat someone up. And often, it's not about, 'can I chat someone up?' But, 'can I shout a comment at someone'.

As within many of the other accounts, an explicit criticism of traditional modes of clubbing masculinities is built into Jane's. She goes on to explain how she views sexual relations within rave and post-rave clubs and claims that she would never have become involved in rave had men not become less predatory and aggressive. She says:

> If men speak to you now, they don't want to pick you up. You can have a nice chat and you can be perfectly into having nice chats. Men are happy with dancing as well now. They're happy doing what the women are doing.

Amy presents a similar picture of the contemporary rave event:

> [Men] seem very unaggressive. They're friendly in a completely different way from people when they're completely pissed-up. The men – even in kind of 'hardcore' clubs – aren't sort of predatory and they're not . . . they don't seem like they're there to pull. You don't get come-ons all the time and there's nothing sort of threatening about the atmosphere, like there is when people are drinking. I mean you do get people making advances in 'E hardcore' clubs but not . . . they seem very unthreatening and they seem to kind

of leave you alone. If someone does sort of approach you, they're not pushy and they don't sort of invade your space and they don't touch you in an unwanted way.

Jane's and Amy's arguments are actually supported by Adam,[1] an 18-year-old man whom I interviewed in 1990, as part of a separate project, and who says that the 'techno, "E" clubs' that he now goes to in and around London, are entirely different from the local clubs and discotheques he used to attend in his own small home-town:

> Rave's different from other clubs I've been to. It's just beer. Disco and clubs – like *that* is beer. Everyone goes up there and it's like a louty sort of thing. Everyone gets pissed, tries to pull a bird – that's what it boils down to. That's what having a good time *is*. It's not like a rave. You go to dance and do your pills and that's what you go for. It don't matter if it's a boy or girl or ... 'cause like everyone's so friendly. It's not about pulling and that. You go and you have a good time and like, you come back. That's it.

Sarah Thornton argues that such descriptions of rave's difference from traditional nightclub cultures actually bear very little relation to reality. For Thornton, the drunken 'cattle-markets' which some of the ravers she spoke with referred to, are merely descriptions which function in the construction of an imaginary 'mainstream'. This argument is perhaps one of the most questionable within her analysis. Almost all of the present interviewees refer, for example, to the 'cattle-market' atmosphere of the kinds of clubs they attended before rave. To cite Jane again for instance:

> There was always the idea when you got approached of oh God, are they going to demand something from me that I'm not going to give – meaning a snog, or a fuck, or a date, or a phone-number, or whatever.

Elaine explains:

> I mean I *did* like going to clubs – always. But I hated all that you know ... that men and women and slow dance and beer. I just went for music but I still never did it that much. Not like I rave.

> It was just something I did kind of . . . like I did it, but hated the bad things about it.

She returns later in the interview to what she means by these bad things:

> I mean it kind of made men and women very different. I just hated all the slow-dance stuff and beered-up men and even though I *did* used to get excited at the thought of going out to a club, that bit of it always put me off and getting hassled and stuff.

To go back once more to Thornton's arguments, although many of these interviewees *are* making sense of rave culture in terms of its difference from a 'mainstream', such distinctions are clearly not functioning simply to construct the self as 'cool' and the scene as 'underground'. Rather, many of these women articulate their experiences of rave, and the pleasures it affords them, in terms of an explicit dissatisfaction with particular forms of masculinity, and particular club scenes which feel like what Jane calls 'pick-up cities'. Whether or not we might want to challenge or question the actual term 'mainstream', in these instances at least, it is obvious that this functions to speak about unpleasant and even potentially dangerous nightclub environments. The term frequently acts then, as a signifier of a sexually oppressive situation from which these women want to distance themselves.

What I believe is a very obvious 'popular' feminism, or what McRobbie calls a 'semi-structure' of feminist feeling, is already apparent from these women's accounts. Commonly, such accounts are based around: (a) an explicit criticism of 'predatory' male behaviour: (b) a language of 'rights' (including the stress on the 'right' to dance unharassed, the 'right' to wear particular clothes without this signalling some kind of sexual invitation, and the 'right' to go out dancing without men) and, (c) an understanding of rave as signalling some kind of 'evolution' in sexual-political terms. Indeed, almost always interviewees over 20 years old, talk about rave in terms of an evolution; a sexual-political 'progress'. And it is not even as though the women need to be asked directly about the sexual politics of rave (although admittedly, they know what my work is about). Commonly, and with no direct prompting, but simply in response to my general question 'what does rave mean to you?', I am offered a critical (and in this sense 'political') story of a sexually progressive movement within club cultures. The language is very clearly a language of 'feminism'. Several (including Jane, Amy, Clare and Jean) actually compare their own opportunities with those of their mothers. Amy says, for instance:

> I remember my mum saying 'Oh you're really lucky, 'cause I used to love dancing, but you couldn't do it without a partner.' And I thought yeah, that's really good. You can dance on your own. You don't need a man to ask you to dance or you don't need anyone to dance with. You don't even need anyone to go to a rave with. It's changing.

In response to a question I pose about childcare, Jean says:

> Well, my mum has him up there 'cause she's happy yeah . . . like she's 'You mustn't just sit indoors all the time just 'cause [Jean's ex-boyfriend's] gone to prison.' Like she's all for it. Like she didn't have the chances herself so she's 'yeah, fine. Go for it. Have a laugh', 'cause she understands right. But she never got that chance herself you see. It wasn't so easy was it? Now it's all right and you're going to be all right in a rave you know.

It is clear that if women are claiming to feel safer, freer and more 'at home' within contemporary nightclub environments, then this has a lot to do with the ways in which clubbing masculinities are seen to have changed. In the absence of 'hassle' from 'predatory' men, these women are freed-up to explore modes of femininity which are based upon both collectivity and self-centredness. Part of this self-centredness is, as Amy points out, about a certain narcissism or what Jane calls an 'autoeroticism' – a 'getting off' on oneself. Rave gives Jane what she calls a 'personal space' within which she feels that she can 'show off' (a term also used by two of the other women). But importantly, certain conditions must be in place for this physical putting 'on show' of the female self (becoming what Jane calls a performance for somebody *else*). For one thing, these women have to feel 'safe'. For another many stress that although they *do* (or sometimes do) enjoy a certain to-be-looked-at-ness within dance events, precisely *who* they are being looked at by, and *how* they are being looked at, matters very much. Finally, many emphasise the point that they do not want such 'performance' to be so unproblematically associated with sexual 'come on'. And rave is seen to be 'positive' in sexual-political terms precisely because the dressed-up, drugged-up, dancing female body is seen to have been wrenched, or at very least loosened up from its long-standing associations with sexual invite. This is fundamentally important for many of these interviewees. Louise, whose account I want to turn to now, tells me:

> I walk around pouting most of the night anyway. It's like me and [her friend], we just walk around and we just like, you know, pout and walk around and stuff. That's the way I dance you know. It's how I like acting you know. And *why not* you know? It's how I like acting you know. Because I'm so dressed up, it's easy to meet people. And I go around giving everyone huge hugs you know. It might be a bit flirty, but there's *nothing* wrong with that and anyone who thinks I'm out to be pulled is wrong. I *hate* it when that's the assumption.

Louise: chaos, glamour and confusion

Louise is 22 and originally from Grimsby, but now living in London where she is temping. She is relatively unusual within the sample as a whole inasmuch as she is heavily involved in DJing, organising rave events and political activity against the Criminal Justice Bill. Louise is one of the founders of a group called 'Subliminal Revolutions' which organises rave events and political demonstrations. As she explains:

> We're just out to mess people's minds up – get them thinking. You know, not just about clubbing but about their whole lives. About you know . . . just trying to stir people into any kind of thinking. These aren't the times to sit around staring at your belly button you know. People have got to start thinking for themselves. Too many people, like you know . . . I do it myself. If there's somewhere cosy where you can go and turn into a vegetable, then you tend to.

She continues:

> People don't question things. They just carry on. It's like stuff around the Criminal Justice Bill. It's like getting in without almost anyone blinking because like, for a start, it's like *that* outrageous that if I tried explaining to people like you know, parents and people you work with, it's so abhorrent that people just won't believe it. It's like 'no, that's rubbish'. They've worked it out so cleverly that it's just so appalling that people just won't believe it's happening. Or if they do, it's like 'well, there's nothing I can do'.

Despite suggesting that in some respects rave culture is politically underdeveloped, Louise does argue that it did bring with it important changes to dance club sexual relations. Sexual divisions and inequalities continue, she says, at the organisational and production levels of this culture, although she believes that these too may now be changing:

> I think that a lot more women *could* get a lot more involved. I mean there aren't that many female DJs – not known as well as the men are. There's a few about, but I mean me and [her female DJ partner] have just started it. In any kind of music it tends to be men that take it on and like ... I mean, women are laughed at basically – quite a lot. And you know the old joke about, women only go to see bands 'cause they fancy the male singer. You know, that kind of attitude. It never occurred to me till about a year ago that I could do it – you know, that I could DJ. So things are changing and I think it's easier you know, for women to do it now.

Louise describes having become a techno DJ within a music industry which is male-dominated and in which women are, she claims, frequently ridiculed, exploited and discriminated against. Rave is seen to have brought about some important changes to this situation. She presents numerous examples of female friends involved within either music journalism or music production and contrasts these environments to rave culture which, although still male-dominated, is, she argues, more progressive in sexual-political terms. As she puts it:

That's the great thing about faceless techno-bollocks. It *is* faceless. It doesn't matter *who*'s making it, *who*'s organising it. You don't have to be a pretty pop star. You don't have to be a sexy pop star. That's one of the great things about it. Like . . . like the rock n' roll thing *is* such an ego thing and it's like trying to be sexy and impress. But when you're trying to get people dancing, it doesn't matter how old you are, or who you are. It's the music that matters.

Interestingly, although Louise stresses the extent to which at the production and organisational levels of rave, female appearance is less important than it once was, at the level of her own participation within events, being able to 'show off' is clearly important. Unlike the senses of self which she experiences within her workplace for example, the rave space is one in which she can safely perform more 'glamorous' ways of being. She describes for instance, wearing 'feather boas and high heels' and repeatedly casts the rave environment as one in which she can do this without encountering the assumption that this signals some kind of 'come-on'.

Louise's stress on the importance of being able to 'dress up' without this leading to 'hassle' is something which many of the other women also speak about. Amy for example, says of raving:

Yeah, it's a 'showy-off' thing as well and probably um . . . sort of . . . I don't know. I say 'showy-off' because E-type clubs are so much more *about* dancing. You watch other people dance and they watch you.

Later on in the interview, Amy explains:

I mean, I *do* like dressing up lots, sort of . . . kind of, I suppose, to shock but also just trend. I used to get quite unpleasant comments. I remember, where was it? Electric Ballroom in Camden I think and getting loads of comments from men, like 'slag' as I walked past. And lots of unwanted attention. Men were just kind of dancing up to me – sort of sexily dancing up to me as though you're obviously there to get laid. I don't really find it like that any more.

Partly, what makes women like Amy and Louise feel able to dress up and dance within a rave event, without attracting unwanted attention, is the fact that such practices are seen to have been somehow normalised and to an extent, even 'de-sexualised' within this context. As Jane explains:

> Dancing sexily ... It's ... But somehow it's sanctioned in a club. 'Cause if you look round you think other people are doing it too so it's ok. It's normalised because like, *everyone* is doing it and you can always see somebody out there with less clothes on than you and dancing way more sexy than you. And all you think is wow, they look like they're having a good time – and it actually helps you to as well.

McRobbie (1994) has written about the emergence within rave culture of what she calls 'hyper-sexualised' modes of femininity and her argument clearly finds support within many of these interviewees' accounts. What such women stress however, is that such a performance is possible, pleasurable and 'safe' precisely because it has come to signify very differently. Emptied of its traditional signifiers of sexual invitation, a 'hyper-sexualised' performance of femininity, can take on new meaning. The enactment of such a mode of femininity has, it appears, become very much an end in itself, instead of being seen as a means to some other end. So several of these interviewees stress heavily the pleasures involved in cultivating a particularly 'sexualised' appearance for no reason beyond the performance itself. And we find within many of these accounts, long and detailed description of the pleasures involved in simply dressing up, or otherwise preparing the self before an event. Chris, Kay, Angie, Sally and Jean all describe taking photographs of themselves before going out to a rave. Sally and Jean actually show me some of these during our interview, and they tell me that they have rented a camcorder to record their preparations for their next rave. For these women, getting ready is clearly just as important as is actually going into a dance event. Like some of the other interviewees (including Amy, Louise, Clare, Chris, Kay and Angie) Sally and Jean speak excitedly and at length about the pleasures of actually preparing to go out raving. Both buy new clothes every time they attend an event. They meet at a particular house and spend up to six hours getting ready – dressing and taking photographs. All of this is done whilst taking the first of their 'speed pills'. This 'bedroom' time is an integral part of their rave experiences. On the one hand the image they present of getting dressed up in their bedrooms is a familiar one. But this is a 'pill-popping' bedroom culture suggesting the extent to which adventures once more closely associated with *the street* have entered a space traditionally perceived to be 'innocent' and 'safe'. And this also suggests the degree to which being able to perform a particular (and otherwise rather unlikely) mode of femininity (which involves being 'adventurous', 'out of one's head', hyper-sexualised and so forth) is often an integral part of rave's appeal. As Chris puts it:

> You get all excited don't you? Like . . . like when you're all together getting ready and sort of dressing up and kind . . . we're all trying on different stuff and just sort of egging each other on and put-ting the music louder and strutting around. Posing really if you're honest.

For such women, it is not simply attending a rave event which is pleasurable, but also the whole performance of an otherwise quite unlikely mode of femininity; a performance which rave culture is seen to make possible. But it is precisely because a 'hyper-sexualised' performance of femininity has been quite radically loosened up from its associations with sexual invite, that it is seen to be so pleasurable.

To-be-looked-at-ness is obviously an important aspect of the pleas-ures which some of these women associate with rave. What is being contested however is the idea that this is necessarily for men, or necessarily to do with being 'picked up'. Women like Louise, Amy, Sally and Jean suggest that this to-be-looked-at-ness has much more to do with being able to frame themselves in a particular 'sexualised' way, or play out a more 'glamorous' mode of femininity, than it does with attracting a partner, or even with being what Jane calls a perform-ance in 'somebody *else*'s eyes'. There is something intensely *self*-centred about such pleasures. Jane speaks about putting on a performance for *herself*. Amy stresses narcissism and the pleasures of being able to 'show off'. Clare talks about getting totally into *herself*. And her emphasis on being self-centred and self-focused within a rave event, is reinforced as she describes (as do Sally and Jean) the ways in which she sometimes tries to avoid her boyfriend's gaze within a rave event.

His gaze 'brings her down', appearing to frame her in a way that she wants to avoid. She explains:

> I feel like he's watching me and I don't know. 'Cause he has accused me of dancing too sexily and he thinks I'm flirting so I either get self-conscious if he's there or I get angry. I hate it if he's staring like that. So I try and dance somewhere where he can't see me.

At the same time, Clare very obviously enjoys being looked at by *certain* people:

> I just love looking around. That's what you do isn't it? It's amazing when you catch someone's eye and they ... they look at you and you look back and ... it can just be for a second but it's so intense. That eye-to-eye that says ... it communicates you're 'up' together and it's ... it's massively intense. And it can be sexy. Yeah, I think it's *very* sexy ... sexy or sexual or something. But that's it. It *is* just a look.

Many of these accounts indicate that although an intense pleasure often attaches to being looked at, it is the looking itself, rather than what this might *lead* to, which is important. Clare suggests (as do Sally and Jean) that her boyfriend will misinterpret what this is all about. He might mistake the 'sexy or sexual or something' for a come-on, where apparently, this is about little more than the pleasures of a particular performance. Clearly, it is not simply being looked at, but also actively looking which is cast within these accounts, as pleasurable. Men and other women become the objects of a gaze which is 'sexual', but in a way which appears to indicate nothing beyond itself. Sally and Jean for instance, in describing their favourite events, talk of 'pit-stopping' where the 'horny men' or the 'willy' are:

> J: It's huge, loads of lights and your lasers and that. Loud music. Thumping music. Loads of willy. Yeah, loads of horny men. I tend to dance where the horniest men are, isn't it?
> S: Yeah, we end up walking through the crowd, and stop ...

J: Yeah, see horny geezers and it's like 'we're here. We'll dance here.'

S: Yeah, I'm behind and it's like a pit-stop where the blokes are.

Despite such talk, few of these interviewees (including Sally and Jean) claim that they ever go to clubs or raves to 'pull'. Indeed, many stress that the club environment is not particularly suited to meeting potential sexual partners – primarily, because one is so *self*-centred within an event, but also because talk is made difficult and further-more, because of a reluctance to leave an event with an unknown man. This is about the immediate pleasures of looking, being looked at, and performing rather than a focus on something lying beyond this. And these pleasures *do* appear as a very central part of rave's appeal to these women. Sally, for example, in describing a particular rave which she did *not* enjoy, puts this down to the fact that 'no men were looking at [her]'. When I ask her to say more about this, she explains: 'No it's not like I'm big-headed right, but when no ... we're like ... when you got no men looking at you, it ain't the same. It is *not* so good.'

Looking and being looked at are then, constructed by many of these women as important factors of the pleasures they experience within an event. These particular 'scopophilic' pleasures are central. For Sally and Jean, watching a 'horny man rush' works to intensify their highs. They tell me, 'It's like whoosh – you're up there.' And Catherine says:

> You could look at everyone and everyone – especially my mates – looked gorgeous. Women and men. They just looked so engrossed in their own bodies and so into the music and almost unaware of anyone else – until they looked up and caught your eye. And it was amazing – like a peak.

Looking and being looked at are thus charged with an intense pleasure which is described as 'sexual' or 'orgasmic' but which does not *lead* anywhere. Instead, these pleasures appear to suggest a kind of almost mirror-engagement – a process whereby the self is reflected back to the self, with the intense gaze from another acting as a mirror confirm-ing and intensifying one's own 'high'. The pleasure thus appears to be about being 'seen', and being able to 'see' oneself, in a particular kind of light – dressed-up, 'out of it', drugged-up, hyper-sexual yet nevertheless somehow 'beyond reach' (insofar as the interviewees frequently stress the extent to which 'E' is seen to put some kind of 'seal' around them.).

To return to and close discussion of Louise's account, her story is a far more recognisably 'political' one. She casts herself as a feminist in describing her work as a DJ within a predominantly male environment – an environment which she very clearly sees herself challenging. On other occasions she speaks of herself as an anarchist – telling me that she identifies with Discordia, the Goddess of chaos. At other times still, she speaks of herself as a hugging, pouting 'flirt'. The rave environment is seen to afford her the possibilities for living out all of these different situations at once. All of these particular performances of femininity afford her senses of self which are very different from the ones which belong within her day-to-day life. Significantly, I interviewed Louise within her workplace and upon meeting me, she immediately tells me 'This is *not* the real me you're seeing now.' The 'real' Louise who emerges within a club world is 'madder', more glamorous, more 'out of control' and more 'chaotic' than she can otherwise be. Indeed, when she invites me to one of her forthcoming events, she explains that at first I may well not recognise her. Like Jane, Louise paints the rave environment as one within which very different performances are made possible. As Jane puts it:

> When you're in work-mode, it's one thing. And when you're in that girlfriend-mode it's one thing. And in a club, it's like mad-mode takes over. When I'm in club-mode it's a different me.

If the present interviewees valorise the 'madness' and 'confusion' which they can experience within the rave environment, then the idea of spreading this madness and confusion is something which Louise – as an increasingly successful club organiser and DJ – has turned into an almost 'political' project. In describing what she feels she is doing with her organisation 'Subliminal Revolutions', she explains:

> I think if you bombard people with enough chaos and make them confused enough, they're gonna have to start thinking. And confuse people enough and they will *have* to start thinking for themselves,

you know.... This is what it's all about. People *do* like that confusion you know, but we're too lazy sometimes. Give them a place for all that chaos and they love it, you know.

Clare: split loyalties, contradictory desires

Clare is a 31-year-old Londoner who is currently unemployed. She has been involved in various different club scenes since the age of 14. Before the advent of rave, Clare went mainly to what she calls 'black funk' clubs in London. She began going to illegal raves in and around London in 1989 and carried on doing this for about two years. After this, she went mainly to House clubs and parties and now describes herself as not a particularly big 'hardcore' fan, telling me that she no longer has the energy for dancing to this kind of music. Although for three years during the mid-1990s, Clare's clubbing became less frequent, she has – over the past two years – gone back to clubbing and raving on a regular basis. At the time of interview, she was attending a variety of House clubs, pay parties and free dance events on a fortnightly basis, using 'dance-drugs' usually, although not always.

One of the most interesting and prominent issues to emerge from Clare's account relates to a tension which she experiences between being a clubber and being involved in a long-term heterosexual relationship. This is what I want to focus upon for now, and in so doing, I want to build upon some of the arguments I have been developing about: (a) changing constructions of 'adult' femininity and: (b) the alternative senses of self which seem to be enabled within the context of the rave.

Very rarely does Clare actually rave with her male partner, and as I indicated earlier, she stresses that when she *has* done this, she has tended to not enjoy the event, or at very least, to not enjoy being within her boyfriend's sight within an event. This is mainly because her boyfriend has more than once accused her of dancing 'too sexily' and of flirting with other men. When I ask if such accusations have ever led to actual arguments she says:

> Oh yeah, more than once 'cause...I don't know. I guess it's 'cause he's never been a clubber, so he doesn't know what it's about. And he just thinks it's about other men or sex or something. It's...it's pathetic really because...just because he can't

see the appeal, he finds it threatening. I mean, he can't see that it's something I've always done and it's important to me. For him, because he doesn't do it, he thinks it's really juvenile and something which means I'm trying to be a teenager. And he thinks being a teenager is about flirting and sex.

Clare's description of her attempts to avoid the watchful eye of her boyfriend within an event (she tells me 'so I try and dance somewhere where he can't see me') parallels a description given by Jean who says that she spends much of her time within an event trying to escape her current casual boyfriend. It is only when she has 'come down' from her pills, that she *then* goes to find him. Jean describes feeling constantly nervous about the prospect of this man seeing her and 'starting a fight'. But it is not simply the prospect of a fight which makes for Jean's avoidance of her boyfriend. This avoidance also appears to be about the extent to which her boyfriend's gaze threatens to disturb how Jean *wants* to be seen and how she *wants* to see herself within an event. If, as I suggested in my introduction, raving can provide a means of entry into an 'elsewhere', then both Jean and Clare construct their male partners' gazes as potential obstacles to this entry. Clare for example, explains that it is not simply her boyfriend's accusations which disturb her, but also how his gaze seems to pin her down to a particular subject position; a position which she is attempting to temporarily move out of:

> With him it's...it's not like being with my friends and going clubbing. He sort of sees me as different and...and it's kind of not so easy to be wild and that around him. I mean, he knows and...and I guess he *does* sort of respect that I have a kind of wild side to me...to my personality, but not in...like he *doesn't* respect it in *that* kind of situation. I feel I have to act differently and not really let go. It's just not so relaxed.

She goes on to explain:

> If he's staring and looking...I don't know. If he's looking at me, I feel it's smirky sometimes like I'm being pretentious and he's telling me that, you know 'This isn't really you Clare.' I just don't feel comfortable with him. That's it I guess. It can ruin a whole

night for me. He doesn't do pills, and he sometimes...Well, *sometimes* he's done a pill, but he's not a big dancer, and he doesn't get into the spirit of it really. It's not him.

Partly, and to pick up on the question of changing stories of 'adult' femininity, which I addressed earlier, what Clare appears to find uncomfortable about her boyfriend's gaze is the extent to which this makes her feel like she is not behaving adult enough or not doing adult femininity 'properly'. As she puts it: 'I know [her boyfriend] doesn't like it. Again, it's me playing at being a kid. But it does mean so much to me and the thought...when I think of losing it, it's depressing.'

In reflecting upon her boyfriend's attitudes towards her clubbing, Clare is consistently critical of the very different ways in which she and he view each other's leisure activities. She repeatedly mentions that whilst she respects her boyfriend's interest in football he, on the other hand, tends to ridicule her interests in clubbing. His football does not make him somehow immature. Clare's clubbing on the other hand, is seen as evidence that she has not yet stopped being 'a kid': 'You know, I really do never call *him* a kid when he's into the whole football thing. It's the opposite. I really respect it.'

For Clare, raving is something which she is now struggling to defend in the light of her partner's derision. And she clearly feels a conflict between wanting to continue her relationship and wanting to continue clubbing. These different situations obviously make for very different (and in some ways, seemingly incompatible) ways of being. To return to Jane: '...When you're in girlfriend-mode it's one thing. And in a club, it's like mad-mode takes over. When I'm in club-mode it's a very different me.'

Clare explains:

> I mean, I adore him but I don't want to spend all my social time with him. I mean, he does loads of stuff with his mates that I'm not interested in, but I don't mind. Like, he goes football every Saturday and I never go with him, 'cause I believe that space is very important. And I've tried making him admit that what I do is no different, but he's not up for it. Maybe...I guess it's 'cause what I do is at night and he's never sure when I'll be home. Maybe *that's* it then.

Clare's account of her rave involvement is thus woven around a set of conflicts or tensions. Being a clubber conflicts with her being within a heterosexual partnership – and Clare tells me that she believes she may not be able to remain a clubber *and* stay with her partner for much longer. Her boyfriend is presented as someone who does not understand why she clubs, does not like the friends with whom she clubs, and who is intensely critical of her drug-taking practices – and she admits to having lied to him on several occasions about the frequency and extent of these. He appears as someone who simply refuses to accept or respect Clare's recreational activities.

It is possible to say that like Jane and Amy, Clare is living a conflict of our times. On the one hand, the space is there for her to club and party. These are becoming more culturally acceptable practices for a woman of her age. Her friends do it and enjoy it as much as she does. Such women are no longer so forcefully hailed by the discourses of domestic enclosure or by the maternal responsibilities which in the past perhaps gave heterosexual women a clearer sense of where their lives were (or should be) going. Clare's boyfriend seems unable to accept her recreational practices as 'appropriate' behaviour for a woman in her thirties. In the absence of a properly established discourse and a recognisable history such practices find little legitimation. It seems that one of the few things that Clare can appear as, within this relationship, is somehow 'immature' or otherwise unable to 'move on'. Within her group of female friends, these practices are normalised. Her friends can share in the image which she entertains of herself within the club environment, but this image is radically questioned when it comes to her sexual partnership with her boyfriend. In this sense, Clare's account raises some very interesting questions about the new spaces into which women are moving, and how these spaces have yet to become meaningful in relation to established norms of heterosexual female being.

If Clare's recreational practices make her look somehow 'immature', then when it comes to her boyfriend's practices, the story is a very different one. He, it seems, faces none of the tensions which she describes. His status as an 'adult' never comes into question. As she puts it, she never calls him 'a kid'. Men have long been afforded the opportunities for an investment in both outdoor 'adventures' *and* domestic intimacy. This dual situation does not bring into question their situations as 'adults'. But it is precisely such questions which women like Clare – as a regular raver – appears to be facing. Perhaps, she suggests, it is the fact that her boyfriend is never sure when she will 'come home' which makes for these tensions. Negotiating these different positionalities involves compromise, confusion and even what she suggests is a certain depression. And such feelings do seem to be centrally related to the fact that Clare is not following a traditional 'life-course' or a traditional 'transition to womanhood'; a journey from 'belonging' within the family home, to 'belonging' within the marital home, with out-of-home recreational pursuits (such as those enjoyed within the nightclub) serving as little more than functional gap-fillers in between. Such a traditional life-course is changing radically. Women like Clare, Amy and Jane are living some of the difficulties which such change brings. And like some of the other women I have so far discussed, Clare imagines that 'motherhood' might be the key to getting her back on a 'proper' path. In 'having' a child, she might stop 'acting' like one.

Like Clare, Jane (who is also involved in a long-term heterosexual relationship) expresses a similar resentment about the fact that her boyfriend's recreational practices are not seen to pose the same kinds of relationship tensions as do hers. She has, she says, been made to compromise. Her boyfriend is in a band and he plays in pubs and other venues. Second to clubbing, Jane's major leisure activity involves following her boyfriend around and watching him perform. She rarely misses one of his gigs. She explains:

> I have compromised. And I'm sure it's got to do with going out with him. He doesn't club at all. He has a band and that takes him into, not a *club culture*, but a *circuit*. And me *too*.

Unlike Clare however, Jane says that she would *like* her boyfriend to club with her occasionally and to show some interest in this. This however, remains unlikely because again clubbing is associated with being juvenile:

> I would like him to club. I'd be really happy if he did. But he doesn't so that's it. When it comes to me clubbing, he doesn't do it. He doesn't give a shit at all. He thinks it's childish.

Both Clare and Jane are located at the intersection of different and as-yet seemingly incompatible discourses. As women they cannot, it seems, be both clubber and 'steady' partner – without this causing tension and difficulty. Being a clubber is in conflict, it seems, with accepted definitions of adult femininity. And to their boyfriends, their failure to leave clubs and raves behind signals a failure to grow up. Clare tells me:

> It feels like I ... Or *he* makes me feel like I'm immature. I think I have to decide between my love life and my social life. It's a pain but I think that's what's coming up for me now

Later on in the interview, she explains:

> It's not like I actually do anything out of order but just that he treats it all like it's really juvenile and it is rubbing off on me – just that lack of respect.

I want to leave discussion of Clare's account for now, and close with what appears to me to be a quite clear summary of the tensions through which she is currently living. Clare will, it appears, have to stop 'losing it', in order to find a clearer way forward with the boyfriend she claims to 'adore' and with whom she obviously wants to continue a relationship. As yet, she remains unsure about precisely how this will happen:

> Well I guess he wants me to settle down a bit, grow up and that way ... I don't know. We *will* want to have children I'm sure and yeah, I guess when I'm more settled down, things will be better between us.

Teresa: a safe space for madness

> I go completely mad. I just lose it. Just totally mad and you *can* be mad. If you did that in a pub, they'd think you were mad. Or if you were at a bus-stop, it would be like, Oh my god, it's a nutter. (Teresa)

Teresa is a 26-year-old woman living in London where she is studying and doing part-time work. She explains that she started going out to clubs when she was fifteen or sixteen but says: 'I really hated the normal clubs that people were going to because it was really shit music and everyone was there to pick somebody up.'

In 1987 she began taking Acid on a regular basis and getting into different kinds of music. In 1989, she started going to illegal raves and she has been raving regularly ever since.

Much of Teresa's account is taken up by the very familiar criticism of certain forms of 'predatory' male behaviour – something which is again associated with pre-rave clubs and alcohol. In describing her first experiences of rave, she says:

> There was no come-on and men weren't trying to pull you either. That made the difference. 'Specially like being a girl, it was horrible when people were just trying to pull you. It was just 'cause they were pissed. It wasn't 'cause they fancied you even. It's 'cause they were just pissed-up and they haven't got anything better to do. But like rave isn't like that.

For Teresa as for all of the other women, what was so appealing about the advent of rave was how this was seen to bring about a 'safe' space for women out to dance and take drugs for the night. Indeed, the criticism of 'threatening' or 'predatory' modes of masculinity is probably the clearest and most consistent theme threading all of these different women's accounts together. This absence is seen to render the rave space a 'safe' one, offering women a somehow secure territory and an impenetrable barrier around this:

> Before I wouldn't feel safe going somewhere like that on my own, because I'd feel intimidated – probably for no reason, but I *would* feel intimidated and I wouldn't feel that I would have people respect my space. Now everyone knows that you've got this certain amount of space around you and no one seems to impinge upon that space. But like that's ... say if someone's drinking you're very aware that they're drinking and you feel sort of, get out of my space 'cause you're drunk and you're all over the place. (Teresa)

> If someone does sort of approach you, they're not pushy and they don't sort of invade your space and they don't touch you in an unwanted way. (Amy)

Yeah, he [her boyfriend] says I dance sexy but that's not really it at all. I mean I find the opposite really 'cause people don't tend to be treading all over you and you've got your own little space. I mean you're close to . . . *very* close to people sometimes but it's not like . . . it doesn't feel like they're trying to get into your space. You have your own space. (Clare)

The ways in which different drugs (namely alcohol and Ecstasy) are seen to make for different spatial organisations of bodies upon the dance floor is something which almost all of the interviewees speak about. Alcohol is seen to make for an invasion of one's personal space, whilst Ecstasy is seen to somehow guarantee a certain 'respect' for this space.

But it is not simply an invasion of, or respect for, *physical* space which these women speak about. Notions of 'safe' space are also built upon the idea or belief that Ecstasy somehow creates a respect for another's 'personal boundaries'. As Kerry puts it:

I think there's a safety net in the feeling that if somebody is on 'E' – if a bloke is on 'E', he will not attack you. He will basically not step beyond whatever boundaries you set. I think it *does* create a sort of safety net.

And Elaine says:

You can stand . . . or you *could* be very close to someone when you're dancing but it feels much safer. It's as if 'E' puts a little . . . like a seal around you.

Having this personal 'seal' or 'safety net' in place is seen as fundamental to the development of the intense senses of community and bonding, which the women repeatedly refer to. Conditions perceived to be in place, a woman can 'let go', 'lose it' and blend into a collective playing out of a kind of ecstatic 'madness'. In this context, she can, as Jane puts it, live out a 'messy side'. From here, she can 'trip' to an 'elsewhere' in which otherwise unlikely modes of being and senses of self can be explored.

'Space' is then, not purely about something physical or material. It is also about having the 'space' within which to be something different.

It is the 'elsewhere' within which different articulations of the body, and alternative experiential worlds can be explored. And if many of these women claim (as they do) to feel 'sad' or 'depressed' about the prospect of having to stop raving, then this is obviously not simply about having to give up a *physical* practice and a *physical* space. This is also about a perceived sacrifice of a certain way of being, and of the imaginary and experiential 'worlds' which develop within the particular assemblage of bodies, drugs, music and space which constitutes the rave event. What is often seen to emerge within such 'worlds' – and Teresa makes this particularly clear – are 'madder', more 'mental' and more 'confused' figurations of female subjectivity (and I shall return to this once more, in the following chapter). 'Settling down' or otherwise stopping rave is, then, seen to be about losing the opportunities for explorations of this kind of being. As Teresa puts it:

> You can really do the maddest things and it's all ... like no one makes you feel mad. Like I can be totally mad and ... and I can't do that anywhere else. It's like Oh my god, I'm going totally mad tonight and you know, I can't ... I don't *ever* want to stop.

> It's like complete and utter madness. That's what I love. I'd find *that* really hard to let go of. (Amy)

> I don't ever want to stop. I don't think we (referring to herself, Kay and Angie) will. There is stuff for older people and we ... we could just go. You'll always find something and I mean, no, I don't want to stop – ever. I will ... I might not go so much, but not stop completely. I can't see myself ... I don't see myself sort of becoming all ... you know, nice and stay indoors and that kind of thing. (Chris)

> I remember my friend saying to me and I think it's true, that you can get off any time, but you can never leave. That even though you say I'm not going or you haven't done it for a while – there's always going to come a point when you do it again. Once you've been there, and once you've been like that, it's hard to leave it permanently. (Holly)

Throughout our interview, Teresa explains that she feels so comfortable within, and so attached to, the rave event because she finds within this a space which is otherwise lacking:

You can be so different to d'you know, to the way I have to be normally. I just know I can't do that other...in other places. You just can't d'you know? It isn't done normally is it? But in a rave I can you know? I can just you know, be very different from normal.

Teresa thus draws a very obvious contrast between how she can be within the rave event, and how she can be 'normally'. And this contrast is woven through the entire account. With people in her 'everyday' world (with her work and college friends for example), she says that she is constantly aware of having to 'act calm'. Otherwise, people will think either that she is 'a nutter' or that she is 'coming on' to them:

'Cause I'm chatty anyway and I talk shit to quite a lot of people (laughs). But if you do that in a pub, or one of the old clubs, people will think you're trying to come on to them, and take it the wrong way. Or even if you're just chit-chatting sometimes you have to keep it a bit more you know, a bit calmer like...like I can just be like myself in a club and I can be *that* mad and it doesn't matter.

In responding to a direct question about the appeal which rave holds for her, Teresa says:

That's it really. I...you know...I'm mad anyway but...but like I can't do it. If you go around doing that – like just letting go like that, people would think I was mad. You couldn't do it. But when I'm raving, you just feel so free and it's like Oh god, I just love this. I just really want to dance and I just want like...*this* is the best night of my life and you know, like *every* night is the best night of your life. It's like pure freedom because there's no control.

Associations between raving and 'losing it' or 'going mad' are, as we have already seen, common throughout these data. Indeed, Louise, in describing her work as a DJ speaks of generating an atmosphere of 'madness' as being almost her 'duty' as an entertainer:

Well, half the people in there are psychotic. It's you know, like wind them up and give them some way of releasing it. Give them some kind of outlet. That's all we wanna do. People *do* come to a rave to be psychotic. We all know that and that's what our job is. To play around with that psychosis.

Although many might put Teresa's 'madness' and her sense of having 'lost' control, down to the effects of Ecstasy, this kind of drug determinist argument is far too simplistic to account for the ways in which she (like many of the other women), celebrates and speaks of what she gets out of an event. For one thing, many of these women do not (or do not always) use drugs, yet they still talk about 'going mental' and 'losing it' within an event. For another, some (like Catherine, Clare, Teresa, Angie, Chris and Kay) have taken Ecstasy in non-rave situations and have not had the same experiences at all. As I have written elsewhere, dance-drug use has to be viewed as part of a much wider and more complex assemblage which includes not only material aspects such as music, bodies, visuals and pills for example, but also the meaning-giving stories or 'texts' generated within (and constituting) rave culture (Pini, 1997a). The 'text of madness' which Teresa draws upon has as much to do with the conditions of possibility for telling particular stories, as it does with the effects of drugs. This is not to downplay the role or effects of drugs like Ecstasy. It is simply to situate these within a much more complicated circuit. To isolate the physiological effects of a drug, would be to ignore the complex context within which such effects happen and come to mean. This is a context within which 'madness' has a particular significance and an obvious appeal. To reiterate, rave encourages and enables, a 'suturing into' the stories of 'madness' and confusion which it generates. But these are not 'stories' as separate from other more material aspects such as chemicals, music and club-decoration for example. All of these aspects are inseparable parts of the 'body' which is rave culture. And what some of these interviewees suggest, is that this 'body' is now more inviting than are traditional sites of female belonging. In other words, what some suggest is that they are being more effectively hailed by stories about 'madness' and 'losing it' than they are by stories about safety, domesticity and stability. I want to close this sub-section on Teresa's account, with an illustration of this. As she puts it:

That's me really. I love going mad and in a rave it's like Jesus, I *can* do this and no one is going to think I'm a lunatic. Oh you know, it's just wonderful. Just totally wonderful that you can do that, and be that...just that 'off it'. Like you can't you know – you can't be like that normally can you?.

Holly, Kerry and Anna: different worlds for adult women

The interview with Holly, Kerry and Anna was the first group interview which I conducted. Both Anna and Kerry are 24 and Holly is 29. Holly and Anna have been raving since its beginning in the late 1980s whilst Kerry has only been raving for one year. The women frequently rave together although Kerry has recently also been going to events with a different group of friends. Holly and Anna rave less frequently than they did up until three years ago (when they were raving on an almost weekly basis). Both decided at this point to take a break (either because they were using too many drugs or because they did not enjoy changes which had taken place within techno-music). They have however, both resumed raving on a relatively regular basis, now attending events at least once every two months.

The three women paint a very familiar picture of contemporary dance cultures and about what they feel they get out of these (stressing aspects such as 'madness', 'self-expression' and being able to 'lose it' within an event). What I want to focus upon for now however, is what the interview says about the relationship between the 'world' of rave and these women's different day-to-day 'worlds'. In short, it becomes clear from the start that a certain self-consciousness or 'embarrassment' marks their conversation. They construct a picture of being situated within two very different (and often incompatible) worlds – the 'world of rave' and the 'day-to-day world'. These 'worlds' are seen to be structured very differently in terms of their social, emotional and linguistic forms. Attempting to make rave intelligible within a non-rave context is seen to be almost impossible. The language does not exist and the emotions would not, they suggest, be understood. Attempting to give form and legitimacy to their rave practices is then, seen as extremely difficult. As Anna puts it:

It's hard you know. You end up using old hackneyed phrases and clichés and that makes it sound embarrassing. Like the words don't really work outside of that context.

I have indicated how almost all of these interviewees valorise the alternative ways of being which they claim to experience within the rave environment. These women say that they can be 'madder', more 'narcissistic', and 'freer' than they can within other spheres of their lives. Such ways of being are, they imply, not allowed, or at very least they are not encouraged within their day-to-day worlds. Holly, Kerry and Anna add weight to such images, as they construct the rave event as one in which what they call 'altered states of consciousness' (Anna) and 'utterly different ways of relating to people' (Kerry) develop. What comes across very clearly here, is the extent to which such different ways of being really do not belong within their wider day-to-day lives. Moreover, talking about these can only make one look embarrassingly 'naff'. In response to my very general initial question about what rave means to them, the women begin the following conversation:

> H: It's a really important part of my life. It's only recently I suppose that I've been thinking about it again. It's quite intense in that the experience is so different from *anything* you've experienced before and it is so nice and friendly.
> A: Do you ever feel embarrassed talking about it like that?
> K: Yeah, fully.
> H: Embarrassed?
> A: Yeah, 'cause you were talking about it in such a positive way like it's been like this really good experience and you loved it, whereas I know when *I'm* talking with certain people, that I feel really embarrassed.
> K: Oh yeah, 'cause it's a totally embarrassing thing to go on about. I tried to describe it to my sister and I felt a right twat.
> A: Yeah, today with one of my colleagues, just vaguely talking about it – 'cause I'd read an article about rave – but I just changed the subject really quickly.
> H: If you listen to yourself, it does sound a bit . . .
> A: Like an old hippy . . . wally. Yeah, you know, it all sounds a bit embarrassing.

Later in the interview, Anna returns to her embarrassment about possibly sounding overexcited. She can behave in an excited, talkative and friendly way *within* an event, but once outside this and reflecting back, she feels 'painfully embarrassed':

> I like talking to people in a place but like...yeah I get into all of that and being very friendly and chatty but usually the next day I think about those people and how I was talking all excitedly and I think oh god, how painfully embarrassing it was getting carried away and talking about it all.

The women thus paint a picture of the rave environment as one which is more friendly, and 'positive' than their day-to-day worlds. They can be more chatty, more sociable, more 'excited', more intense and what Holly says is 'more optimistic' within this environment. The experience is, as Holly puts it 'so different from *anything* you've experienced before'. But, within a non-rave context, talking about such experiences is bound, they believe, to sound 'naff'. Indeed, they all tell stories like Anna's of deliberately stopping themselves from talking about these experiences to non-ravers, or to people outside the rave context. They would, they agree, only sound like 'twats', 'hippies' or 'wallies'.

If the women feel embarrassed by talking about being within a rave, then this is about more than simply a fear of appearing 'uncool'. Although there clearly *is* an element of this here – an awareness of how 'uncool' it is to put into words, let alone to 'go on' about raving – this embarrassment also has a lot to do with their perception of the everyday world as one in which open displays of friendliness and excitement are either lacking or considered somehow 'uncool'. Like the ravers who Barbara Bradby references, the rave is constructed here as a warm and friendly community standing in quite stark contrast to the day-to-day world. As they talk, the women ask themselves why they might be embarrassed:

A: But I wonder why it *is* embarrassing.
K: 'Cause we're conditioned to not say nice things to one another.
H: You're not really supposed to be like that, and if you *are*, it's embarrassing.
K: It's not really the way you're encouraged to be towards people. You're just not conditioned to be that friendly and nice towards others, are you?
H: No.

Being friendly and positive are potentially embarrassing outside the rave context. What I have elsewhere referred to as rave's 'text of positivity' (Pini, 1997a) does not work here. And the kinds of selves which are articulated in terms of this text, can be nothing more than 'naff' or 'uncool' outside the rave context or in a context made up of non-ravers. At one point in our conversation, Anna (who appears most concerned with how 'uncool' her excitement might sound) reminds Kerry (who seems least prepared to 'give into' a perceived cultural pressure to stop talking 'excitedly') of how 'naff' she sounds when 'going on'. Kerry tells her:

> I know, but no, you *won't* destroy my positivity – not totally. I know what it all sounds like and I'm only saying it because we're here now talking about it but I mean I *know* how it sounds.

In response, Anna says:

> No, I don't want to destroy it, but it's like a bit of an embarrassing thing to admit to. You know, it does sound a bit naff and that, to be going on about things being so nice and I just try to not do it.

Clearly, much could be said about these women's references to a subcultural capital hierarchy in relation to which a 'positive' and seemingly 'overexcited' take on rave culture would appear 'naff' or 'uncool'. Trying to put raving into words risks, as Sarah Thornton argues, dissolving the mysterious attitude called 'hip' which youth cultures work to generate. But there is a lot more to these women's accounts than simply an attempt to appear 'cool'. For one thing, particular notions of a 'cool' detachment (which is usually associated with masculinity) are frequently explicitly challenged here. Kerry for example tells the following story:

> Yes, there was that time in Camden at the Lock and all the bouncers were over on the other side of the water thinking that they had the whole situation under control. But no. It was really funny because people were jumping in and actually swimming and completely overthrowing them basically. They didn't stand a chance and it was all rather funny really because they do act rather big and hard don't they? They're a bit of a joke. They completely lost

control. It was hysterical really. I do like seeing them brought down a rung or two. They can be very into themselves, and it's good to see them looking . . . well, looking not quite so cool.

This construction of the rave bouncer as a 'bit of a joke' is not peculiar to this particular interview. Many of the other interviewees (including Clare, Sally, Jean, Chris, Kay, Angie, Louise and Jane) also present at least some criticism of 'cool', 'moody' or 'hard' men who do not 'let go' or 'let off' and who are seen to embody 'attitude'.

Secondly, these women do not appear to be embarrassed so much by their experiences within a rave as they do by attempting to give sense to these within their wider lives. And it appears that this is not simply because 'overexcitement' is 'naff', where youth cultures demand a certain 'cool'. What the interview also suggests is the extent to which the women recognise that not only might they sound 'uncool' but they may also appear juvenile. The particular kinds of excitement and positivity of which they speak, are viewed as being somehow inappropriate for adult women to be feeling. This is made particularly apparent by Anna who is a teacher. One of Anna's greatest fears is that she might be seen by a pupil or a colleague when raving. She thus takes steps to avoid events held in certain areas where her pupils might be. She would, she explains be 'horribly embarrassed' were she to be seen raving by a pupil. But, it is not only her pupils whom she speaks about wanting to avoid. And her wanting such avoidance is not simply because being seen raving by a pupil might undermine her position as a teacher. Anna (and here both of the other women agree with her) stresses, that being seen as a raver (and not just by people known to her) would simply undermine – in very general terms – her status as an 'adult'.

K: Yes, it's not just like embarrassing is it, it's all just a little bit childish. I mean . . .
A: I know what . . .
K: I don't *feel* that. Not really, but that's how it can *look* you know.
H: You mean kind of coming across as a bit juvenile?
A: Exactly. You know, it's OK for so long. I mean when I was younger it didn't really matter so much but . . .

K: And now you enjoy it less?
A: No, not necessarily, but I think it's something more under-standable for a younger person to be doing.

Although all three women appear to share the view that raving is likely to be seen as a somehow juvenile practice, it is Anna who appears most concerned about this. And I want to suggest (albeit very tentatively) that Anna's concern is perhaps so strong because (and unlike almost all of the other interviewees who are either unemployed, studying or doing temporary work) she has, (at the time of interview) a clear career-path before her. And this appears to make a difference to the story which she presents. Admittedly, it is perhaps no more than coincidence that one of the two interviewees who has a career which she enjoys being involved in, is also the interviewee who appears least invested in rave culture and who is most 'embarrassed' by speaking about, and identifying with, this culture. Although she says that she still enjoys raving, Anna seems far less connected to a 'raver' identity than do her two friends. Indeed, she constructs herself as having very much let go of such an identification. It belongs in her past. She explains, 'you see I used to be like that, but not any more'. For Anna rave is something she did as a 'kid' (a term which appears to refer less to her age, and more to her previous situation as a student). Her account (although and to reiterate, it is very hard to draw out from a single woman's claims) *does* suggest that perhaps because she has a stable and long-term career in place, rave comes to play a far less significant role within her life. She is, for example, far less inclined to construct rave as somehow filling a gap in her life. She has few problems imagining giving up rave and her account is marked by none of the 'sadness', 'depression' and so forth which accompany some of the other women's thoughts about changing their recreational practices. And unlike many of the other interviewees Anna does not say things like 'I never want to stop' (Clare) or to make statements like the one I cited earlier by her friend Holly who says:

I remember my friend saying to me and I think it's true, that you can get off any time, but you can never leave. That even though you say I'm not going or you haven't done it for a while – there's always going to come a point when you do it again. Once you've been there, it's hard to leave it permanently. (Holly)

If Holly claims that she will find it hard to leave raving behind permanently, and if Teresa asks 'after that, what *is* there?' Anna seems to be pressed by no such questions. Perhaps this is partly because a 'next stage' is here and clearer for her.

Michelle: anti-CJB political action

Michelle is in her early 30s. This interview was rather different from the others because I conducted it with a colleague and because we focused primarily upon rave culture as a 'resistant' political movement. We therefore dealt less with some of the more direct questions about subjectivity and identity which I focused upon with other interviewees. But I *did* want to include the interview as part of this analysis, because it offers a different angle on the issue of female involvement within rave culture.

Michelle is a co-founder of the Advance Party, a group which organises political activity against the Criminal Justice Bill (CJB). She has been involved in the rave scene for four years and sees this involvement very much in terms of a wider oppositional political movement which involves road protesters, 'new-age travellers' and 'freedom to party' campaigners. In describing her involvement with rave (and she is far more involved with a 'free party' circuit rather than with 'pay parties' or events held in clubs), Michelle is describing a 'political' history. Her account is structured as a description of the many forces which have attempted to prohibit rave and the many counter-movements which have developed to challenge this. Michelle's own work includes the production and distribution of information about the CJB and as a result of this work she has been involved in numerous confrontations with police, one of which ended in her arrest and the confiscation of all of her leaflets. Nevertheless, Michelle continues organising free parties, distributing leaflets and gathering information about government moves to introduce the CJB. Where she organises events, this is very much about a political commitment to developing a safe and non profit-making party scene.

In many respects, Michelle's involvement in rave, is very similar to Louise's. Both women see their roles as politically 'resistant'. Both describe being outraged by government attempts to intervene in rave culture and both work to raise awareness of, and action against these attempts. And both are concerned to provide a safe party space for women. This is something which Michelle very much stresses as she details the various policies put in place to safeguard women within events which she has had a part in organising. She describes, for instance, the forthcoming introduction of a door policy whereby any unaccompanied woman who might appear 'out of her head' is watched as she leaves an event. Taxi number-plates are to be recorded, so that women are less likely to enter taxis which cannot later be identified. Michelle also stresses that within events which she has organised, anybody appearing to be sexually harassing a woman is immediately asked to leave. This is something which is constantly watched for, not simply because it might make female participants uncomfortable, but also because it goes against a general spirit of 'solidarity' which she says should characterise a rave event. She works then, to create an atmosphere which is not just safe, but which is also seen to be radically different from, and critical of, a wider social condition which is seen to be structured around consumerism, profit-making and sexual divisions.

Angie, Chris and Kay: new 'rites of transition'

Angie is 19 and both Chris and Kay are 21. All three women come from London and they all rave together, using a variety of 'dance-drugs' each time they attend an event (all insisting that they would not rave 'straight'). Angie and Kay are sisters and Chris is a long-term friend of both.

The women start their accounts making a familiar association between raving and 'freedom'. In response to my initial question about why they enjoy raving, the following conversation begins:

A: It just lets you go mad – like totally lose it . . .
K: Yeah, you just let go don't you?
A: Yeah, and I mean . . .
C: You can go totally nuts and . . . and you just give it . . . like when you're really 'on one', you don't think about anything else. Like it's you're right up there, just giving it everything . . .
A: You're just really free and your head's free. There's nothing like it. For me, there's nothing like it. I can't handle it if like . . . if I can't go and I miss one.

Chris and Kay have been raving for three years and Angie has been raving for one. I want to draw out two interrelated themes in particular from their account. The first concerns the extent to which these women very much present themselves as a 'girl group' in which care and 'looking out' for each other are fundamental. The second concerns the ways in which 'becoming a raver' is constructed as a kind of 'passage' or a 'transition'.

Throughout the interview all three women emphasise the importance of caring for each other within the rave environment. Not only do they present themselves as each other's 'carers' but (and this is particularly true of the two older women) on occasions they actually present themselves as each other's 'teachers'. Repeatedly, they stress how much they have learnt from each other and from other female friends – about particular clubs, about drug-effects and the management of these, about potentially 'dodgy' men, about music and about 'safe' and 'unsafe' events. From early on in the interview, the two older women thus present themselves as 'carers', guiding and teaching Angie:

> A: Yeah, well it was them (referring to Chris and Kay) who got me into it.
> K: Only 'cause we knew you were coming with *us* though, and we knew you'd be all right.
> C: And you would have got into it anyway with Bob and Jim and it's best . . . you're much safer with us. That's for sure.
> A: Yeah, right.
> K: And I knew . . . I knew at least I'd keep an eye if you popped anything. Like you wouldn't have had a clue what you were swallowing if we . . . you know, if we weren't there.
> A: Yeah, like . . .
> C: Nah, that's true. It's best to be with a mate first time you pop something. Just in case.
> A: Yeah, I reckon I'd have freaked a bit that first time.

This theme of care continues throughout the account, with the 'first time' being constructed as a kind of 'rite of passage' which requires that a certain guidance be at hand 'just in case'. This 'passage' is assisted by the two older women who have already 'been there' and who know what to expect. Indeed, the older women construct their own 'first time' in similar terms, stressing how important it was that they had more experienced friends around during this. Chris says:

> I was really lucky to have Jay with me. She knew what to tell me, about water and stuff. And she was like right there for me and keeping an eye out and every so often – like now and then – she came and got me to see I'm alright. I was really lucky to have her with me 'cause like . . . 'cause she knew where to get some good pills and she knew what to tell me about like water and stuff and to see I was alright and I'm like 'thank you'. I love you mate.' And it was . . . I mean it was like she'd said. But I was glad she was with me.

Interestingly, this description is extremely similar to one given by Sally and Jean who also stress how important their female friends have been in acting like 'guides', teaching them about what to expect from a rave and from drugs. Again, the 'first time' (raving on 'E') is very much constructed as a kind of 'rite of passage'. Below Sally and Jean describe Sally's 'first time'. Jean was at this point more experienced, and occupies a position of guide or carer. Sally begins by explaining how her 'E' affected her and goes on to explain how much Jean helped her in dealing with this:

> S: And I started feeling a bit sick and it was like 'Phew, get to grips.' But I just kept telling myself what Jean had told me beforehand when we've talked about stuff – when she told me the first time she really came-up on an E, how it shocked her. So I kept telling myself this. In the end I came out of it and I just enjoyed it. I just went with it, but it was scary.
> J: And you was well off your head. I thought fucking hell, she's taken a *whole* E and she'd only done like a few halves before 'cause she's always been into Speed. And then she says 'right' when she's been given the whole E. I thought fucking hell, you've done a whole E. Shit! And then she asked me to go by the fire and I thought it's 'cause she's cold. But she *needed* me. I didn't realise she *needed* me.

Later on, Sally also talks about other friends who looked out for *her* when she began raving on a regular basis:

When I first got into them [raves] and started getting into drugs, I was around a lot of older people who sort of looked out for us younger people. You've got to have friends around you to make sure.

Jean, as the person who initially introduced Sally to raves and Ecstasy, now takes up an almost 'proud' position in relation to Sally's 'progress'. She says:

She's *excellent*. In her first year of raving she's done *more* and been *more places* than what *I* did. I just did *Seductions* in Margate – just the Kent places you know. But in her first year, we've been to Milton Keynes – everywhere you know. She's got *right* into it.

Chris and Kay too, adopt an almost 'proud' position in relation to Angie's 'development':

K: Yeah, there's no stopping her now she knows what it's like, right.
C: Right little raver now, she is. (laughs)
A: You can talk. *You* two. (laughs)
K: Yeah but . . .
C: No, right remember your first time – you *never* thought you'd be getting into it all and *now* look at you. You had *no* idea.
K: She's worst than us now (laughs)
A: Yeah, I reckon!
K: She's dead if she's not out blowing it up Saturday night. Right non-stop, *you* are. (laughs) She's pills and the lot.
C: And it's all down to us. (laughs)
A: Yeah, cheers!
C: Go on, you *love* it.

To reiterate, the 'first time' is thus constructed as a sort of 'right of passage' into an unknown world. Later in the interview, Angie describes having never imagined what it would be like to rave 'on E'. Chris and Kay are seen to have assisted her passage into this previously unknown place and experiential world.

A: Yeah, well it's great ain't it? You have ... like you have no idea what it's gonna be like. Even though I knew. They told me what they were ... like I knew what *they* said about it all, and the raves and that. But when they took me and I did a pill – on the first time, that was it. It was like ... Like it was just so mad and great, and then I knew what they were going on about. And they kind of did all the things for me and I was like ... I wanted to walk here and they took me. And I wanted to walk there, and they took me. They just kind of knew how I was feeling and they did it for me.

This theme of care emerges not only in relation to drug-taking, but is also something which very much marks the women's concerns about sexual safety within an event:

A: Yeah, like you make sure you clock it if like ... like even if I'm 'out of it', I can still clock it if like a mate's chatting with some bloke and he's trying to get her to leave or go off.
K: Nine times out of ten, it's just for a spliff or for a chat but ...
A: But you can't be sure, can you?
C: No, we always stick together more or less. It's like you always come back to find each other

This particular account is thus threaded through with a general theme of female care and solidarity. The women are only too aware of the potential dangers which face them when they are on drugs. Although all repeatedly stress the pleasures of 'losing it' within an event, it is clear that this does not mean losing sight of potentially dangerous situations.

The account also suggests the familiar criticism of certain forms of 'predatory' male behaviour which I have repeatedly touched upon. Not only is the 'pissed-up' man seen to be potentially 'threatening', but he is also seen to disturb or ruin what is an otherwise 'good trip'. Chris explains:

I was 'on one' and fine at that and when that bloke came up ... like usually it's all right and friendly. But like he was pissed-up and when he came up, that was *it*. I couldn't get back 'on one'. Later I did, but I had to go outside and ... 'cause I started getting a bit panicked and worried, like you do sometimes.

Although Angie, Chris and Kay are all heterosexual (and Angie and Kay are in relationships with men although in both of these cases, these appear to be very on/off) all suggest a very strong identification with their 'girl group'. Again, none of these women rave with their boyfriends (although Kay used to with her ex-boyfriend and she says that she enjoyed this). And again, the trace of some tension between being a raver, and being within a 'steady' relationship with a man, emerges from the women's accounts. Kay says:

> I wouldn't have fun with him if he came. I've never done an E with him either. I wouldn't like it, you know. It's not the same is it? I'm better with the girls 'cause like they know. You know, they *know* what I'm like and ... Say something went wrong like if ... I'm better off with them, and I can see him ... Like see him on the other nights of the week.

Like Clare, Kay prefers to rave with her female friends. Raving with her boyfriend would not be fun and significantly, she later says that her regular rave activities are partly responsible for their frequent 'splits'. As she explains it:

> He's more like go out for dinner and stuff and even go to the pictures and that or ... or even a drink down the pub. But he's not into this. Yeah, I've just got fed up with it sometimes and thought like ... yeah, like fuck it, this is crap.

Interviewees such as Jane, Clare, Sally and Jean, Chris, Kay and Angie, thus construct raving as something which is very much associated with their all-female groups of friends. In these cases, raving appears as a practice which takes place beyond or outside the world of their heterosexual partnerships. In many ways, it seems to be about escaping this world and finding a safe, intense and pleasurable personal territory beyond. Such constructions indicate a radical departure from traditional views of the nightclub as a place where young women go in the hope of initiating some kind of heterosexual relationship. Today, it is often quite the opposite. Many of the present women knowingly and deliberately exclude their male partners or casual boyfriends from their practices as ravers. And many stress how although they may like talking to, looking at, and being looked at by men within an event, there is a personal 'line' or 'boundary' beyond which men are expected not to go. Rarely is this about a sexual 'pick-up'.

Of course, it would be foolish to make too much of this – to read such examples as evidence of some kind of 'separatism' on the part of young women. It would be equally wrong to suggest that none of the present interviewees enjoy raving with men – whether friends or boyfriends. This really is not the case. But the data *do* very clearly suggest some kind of withdrawal by women from traditional heterosexual organisations. It *does*, in other words, suggest the extent to which women today are seeking out and finding spaces for expressivity and autonomy beyond the normative structures of prescribed femininity, masculinity and heterosexuality. There is a new kind of independence and autonomy here. Indeed, it is precisely this kind of autonomy which some of the women believe upsets their male partners. Clare for example, says in explaining her boyfriend's condemnation of her practices:

> You know, sometimes I think it's not men but my mates that he's jealous of because we all get ready together and get ourselves a bit excited I suppose. I think he gets jealous because he knows they'll do things with me that he can't.

Clare's boyfriend considers her 'juvenile'. But perhaps this is not *simply* because she attaches so centrally to practices and places which might appear more suited to teenagers, that is, dance and dance cultures. Maybe, this reading of her as 'juvenile' is also bound up with her failure to identify more centrally with her heterosexual partnership, an identification which has long been basic to our understandings of how adult heterosexual femininity is formed and defined. She says 'I mean I adore him but I don't want to spend *all* my time with him.' She believes, she says, that 'space is very important' and this appears to be part of how she understands their problem.

I want to leave Chris, Angie and Kay's account with an extract from the start of the interview. Here, the women are talking about rave and boyfriends and they touch upon a theme which emerges from many of these accounts. This concerns the way in which raving is constructed as a practice which takes place outside heterosexual relationships:

A: With [her casual boyfriend] I don't go raving with him. It's different if we're like partying at home or doing stuff like that, but I don't really need him to come raving with me. I mean . . .

K: Yeah, it's not that much fun 'cause you always think about them. You think and you don't really switch off so much . . .

A: Yeah . . .

K: I mean, when I used to with [her ex-boyfriend] it was good but I don't know. It wasn't such a laugh. Sometimes it *was* good, but . . . but I think it's always good with these two. I mean now . . . now like, I like doing things with [her current boyfriend] the next day, say. Like if we go for a drink or something. Like that's good . . .

C: Plus the nooky. Excuse me. [Laughs]

K: Yeah, right. Yeah, that's true though. I do like that when I'm coming-down. (Laughs)

C: Same with me. I used to like that with (her ex). Like not . . . like we . . . we would meet up on the Sunday night or something and I'd still be a bit you know, buzzy and . . . like all a bit high and mellow and that together. That bit's good. . . .

Conclusions

I opened this chapter posing several interrelated questions. Broadly, I set out to examine what the accounts of these women can be seen to say about changing modes of femininity. In particular, I have sought to explore what the accounts tell us about post-feminism, about female experiences of aging, about contemporary articulations of female subjectivity and about the 'alternative' experiential worlds seen to be opened up within the club or rave environment. In this brief concluding section, I want to reiterate some of the arguments I have been building. These are developed further in the following two chapters.

One of the most visible signs of the 'semi-structure' of feminist feeling which McRobbie writes about, comes in the form of these women's repeated condemnations of particular forms of 'predatory' masculinity. In every case, these experiential accounts are woven around a criticism of the sexist, oppressive, or even potentially threatening modes of masculinity which are seen to characterise gig, pub or pre-rave dance cultures. Whether this criticism comes in the form of a direct condemnation of 'letchy' men within an event, or as a reaction against the ways in which women are marginalised within the contemporary techno-music industry, one thing is clear. This is the emergence within the stories of raving women of a clear and consistent challenge to traditional sex relations. This challenge is built into all of these accounts. Indeed, the very basics of rave's appeal are commonly articulated in what are very clearly 'feminist' terms. Almost always, in response to the very general question about this appeal, I am offered a critique of 'pick-up cities' and 'cattle markets' in which 'pissed-up', 'letchy' men are 'out on the pull'. The very definition of what is 'good' about rave culture commonly rests firmly upon the notion of some kind of sexual-political progress. (Amy reminds herself for example, how much easier it is for her to club than it was for her mother. And Clare argues that with rave, the situation for clubbing women definitely changed for the better). Running alongside such challenges is (within many although not all of these accounts) the construction of a much more sexually active and desiring female subject. They may not rave in order to 'pick up', but these women are in no way embarrassed or shy about casting men as sexual ojects who please them, intensify their 'rushes' or otherwise turn them on. Nor are they shy when talking about publicly enjoying the intense 'autoerotic' or 'self-centred' sensations often associated with raving, or about the extent to which raving is often seen as something which exists very separately from heterosexual relationships. A new 'post-feminist' language is so consistent, so familiar and so common across these accounts that it indicates how speaking 'feminist' concerns is simply part of what it now means to speak as a woman. Feminism and femininity no longer appear as the clear and distinct categories they might once have been.

If a form of feminism is suggested by these women's criticisms of 'predatory' men, then it is also evidenced by the language of 'rights' which they adopt in discussing their practices. The 'right' to dance unharassed by men, the 'right' to wear 'sexy' clothes, the 'right' to go out without their male partners, the 'right' to have their recreational practices respected as valid and meaningful, the 'right' to personal 'space' within an event and in short, their 'right' to get 'out of it' (whether this means temporarily getting out of their heterosexual relationship, getting out of their homes, or getting 'out of' their heads) are all aspects which are ongoingly defended and celebrated.

This defence of their 'freedom to party' is then, also about asserting the 'right' to be able to 'lose it' and 'go mental' within a dance event. And I have suggested that in part at least, it is maybe precisely because rave provides entry or passage into some kind of 'mad elsewhere', that it comes to be so significant and appealing to women today. The opportunities for a public playing out of 'madness' and 'loss' may be particularly important at a time when more broadly, femininity's 'life-course' is becoming more and more uncertain, or where the meaning of femininity is becoming more and more fluid. 'Losing it' – whether we are referring to a traditional landmark of femininity or to the act of getting 'out of one's head' – is a sign of our times.

Many of these interviewees claim to find 'home' within 'madness', and belonging within chaos. Fictions from the 'world' of contemporary dance cultures – wherein 'madness' is normal and wherein the incitement to 'lose it' is intense – appear to be more seductive to women to whom traditional stories of femininity no longer appear particularly coherent. If such stories are no longer so effective in suturing the female subject, then within the alternative 'world' opened up by rave, it appears that more inviting, meaningful and seductive fictions are coming to be generated.

But, and to reinforce the point, I am not suggesting that this says *everything* that could be said about women's attachments to rave cultures or that my reading is anything more than partial – one of many possible interpretations. I *do* however, believe that it is more than simply coincidence that this valorisation of 'madness' and 'loss', this stress on 'self pleasure', this celebration of new kinds of 'community' and this emphasis on autonomy, emerge at a time when in more general terms, femininity is being so radically reworked and reconstructed and where as a result, many women experience both 'confusion' but also a certain 'freedom' to explore new ways of being. The rave event appears to provide one important cultural space for such explorations and also, one version of a resolution to some of the contradictions currently surrounding femininity. Here, women are finding an autonomy and expressivity outside established heteronormative structures. They are exploring and living fictions beyond those centred around 'safe' and enclosed 'good' girls.

In the following chapter, I want to take a closer look at precisely what different kinds of stories, figurations of subjectivity and different experiential worlds are emerging from the accounts of these raving women.

Note

1   Adam was interviewed as part of a project looking at the sexual politics of early British rave culture. *See* Pini, 1997a.

4
Cyborgs, Nomads and the Raving Feminine

It is *as if* some experiences were reminiscent or evocative
of others: this ability to flow from one set of experiences to
another is a quality of interconnectedness that I value highly.
Drawing a flow of connections need not be an act of appropriation. On the contrary: it marks transitions between communicating states or experiences. Deleuze's work on lines of
escape and becoming is of great inspiration here; nomadic
becoming is neither reproduction nor just imitation but
rather emphatic proximity, intensive interconnectedness.
Some states or experiences can merge simply because they
share certain attributes. Nomadic shifts designate therefore
a creative sort of becoming; a performative metaphor that
allows for otherwise unlikely encounters and unsuspected
sources of interaction of experience and of knowledge. (Rosi
Braidotti, 1994, p. 5)

In this chapter, I want us to imagine. I want us to think of the images
which emerge from the accounts of raving women *as if* these constituted popular refigurations of the world and subjectivity within this:
refigurations which parallel some of the fictions currently being
mapped within a sphere of contemporary feminist philosophy. The
aim is to consider the extent to which rave – as a lived social practice,
and female ravers – as embodied cultural subjects, resemble the kinds
of formations being imagined by philosophers Rosi Braidotti and
Donna Haraway in their strategic construction of particular Utopias and
political fictions. In short, I want to suggest that rave can usefully be

155

considered in parallel to these often heady philosophical debates – as constituting a popular cultural reframing or refictioning of the world; a reframing which problematises the same dualisms and conceptual frameworks currently under attack from this body of philosophy. In particular, I shall concentrate upon the resonances which such popular cultural visions can be seen to have with Braidotti's 'Nomadic Subject' and Haraway's 'Cyborg'. The chapter is therefore an attempt at bringing into communication the contemporary cultural practice of raving with a particular body of contemporary philosophical inquiry. It is about mapping parallels, resonances and connections between the two.

Why turn to figurational feminism in a study of dance cultures? This is not an unproblematic move I know. But such work *does* suggest some new ways of looking at what raving women say about their practices and also, at what this might indicate about the transformations which femininity is currently undergoing. The work of Haraway and Braidotti points to one way of exploring not simply cultural practice, but also cultural *hopes*, *visions* and a cultural *imagination*. It encourages us to recognise and address the fantasmatic dimensions of these interviewees' personal accounts and of the different experiential worlds into which these women claim to move when raving. For me, this work therefore suggests a way of stepping beyond some of our preoccupations with the distinctions between the 'real' and actual and the 'Utopian' and fictional. As Constance Penley writes in addressing Haraway's work:

> Most Utopian schemes hover somewhere in between the present and the future, attempting to figure the future as the present and the present as the future. (1991, p. 8)

The work to which Penley is referring, suggests a radically different understanding of the relations between the visionary and the 'objective'. And for the purposes of the present, it encourages an alternative approach to questions about the 'credibility' of raving women's experiential accounts. I therefore want to step for a moment beyond any concerns with how 'true' such accounts might be, and consider instead, what these are saying about the present, the future, the visionary and the as-yet-unknown. Clearly, this is not about turning away from the real or the actual. It is about drawing out the visions and fantasies informing and emanating from this reality.

Bradby (1993) argues that Haraway's ideas function better as a political myth than as an epistemology of personal identity and she is correct. Here, I am not talking about personal identity so much as I am referring to a visionary fiction which appears to be threaded through the accounts of the different women I interviewed. The material and discursive assemblage which makes up rave culture can be seen to include a particular, historically and culturally specific version of subjectivity-in-context. Rather than viewing rave as somehow embodying 'meaninglessness' (Reitveld, 1994) and instead of viewing the dancing body generally as a form of physical and hence pre-linguistic expression (Thomas, 1986), this analysis starts from the premise that rave 'speaks'. It may not be 'saying' just one thing, but nevertheless, it 'speaks'. One of the things it 'says', is that embodied female subjectivity can be *otherwise*. Bringing the raver into communication with the figures of the Cyborg and that of the Nomad illustrates, I believe, the extent to which the drive to reinterpret the world does not belong exclusively within the realm of high philosophy, or more generally, within the realm of written or verbal language. But drawing a flow of connections between the raver, the cyborg and the nomad, is not about appropriating the raver into the arms of high theory as if suggesting that she were *actually*, or that she were somehow *the same as*, Haraway's Cyborg or Braidotti's nomad. Instead, and in Braidotti's words, it is about drawing an otherwise unlikely flow of connections intended to make manifest something about contemporary cultural visions and contemporary cultural fantasies about both the present and the future. Here, the female raver, like the Cyborg and the nomad is considered to be involved in a wider staking-out of new possibilities for being-in-culture.

In writing about new feminist figurations, Braidotti argues:

> As Donna Haraway put it, we need feminist figures of humanity that 'resist literal figuration and still erupt in powerful new tropes, new figures of speech, new terms of historical possibility. For this process, at the inflection point of crisis, we need 'ecstatic speakers'. (1990, p. 8)

If we view the current interviewees *as if* they were 'ecstatic speakers' or *as if* they were what Braidotti calls 'myth makers' then what kinds of tales are these storytellers weaving?

Dancing 'out of it'

I started this book talking about contemporary visions of 'elsewheres' and by indicating the extent to which the current interviewees often speak of raving as providing entry into what is commonly described as a completely different 'world': '[Rave's] utterly different to everything else. It's a completely different world. It's like nothing else.' (Clare)

'Unescorted' women have taken to the social dance floor in unpre-cedented numbers. 'Adventures' and 'trips' no longer belong so exclusively to men. Women are now enjoying their own adventurous journeys through the night. These journeys are both physical and they are 'mental' – inasmuch as this is often a 'trip' which does not entail any actual bodily movement. When they speak about this different world, these women are, then, not simply talking about a physical or material space. They are also referring to different ways of being and seeing which the rave event is seen to make possible. As Anna, Kerry and Holly describe it:

> A: You just go off on your own little adventure.
> H: Yeah, have a little adventure.
> A: Yeah, I think when you rave, you go off on your own little trip quite a lot.
> K: You just wander off. You know. It's tripping.

The kind of wanderings described by these women are obviously not entirely peculiar to *contemporary* club cultures. As Helen Thomas's (1993) work illustrates, dance is very commonly experienced by dancers as involving a movement into 'another dimension': a dimension within which what Andrew Ward (1993) suggests are different desires, alternative erotic possibilities and otherwise unlikely relationships can be explored. Indeed, as a concept 'The dance' has been appropri-ated by a number of feminist and other philosophers as a metaphor by which to signal alternative, non-phallocentric images of subject-ivity. Luce Irigaray for example, poses 'The Dance' as an alternative to Freud's concept of the 'fort da' game, suggesting that this is a better way in which to understand the female child's staking out of her own subjective territory in relation to the mother (1989, orig. 1978). For Irigaray, the concept of 'The Dance' serves to get at a form of subjectivity which is not structured around separation and identity. As opposed to the 'fort da' game which involves the casting away and recapturing of a ball of string, and hence the symbolic playing out of the development of subjectivity in terms of a linear, backwards and forwards motion – which signals an attempt to control loss – 'The Dance' is called upon to signal the formation of feminine subjectivity in terms of a set of gestures which are based on gyrations and circularity. This 'Dance' puts the female child in touch with the cosmic, maternal world whilst at the same time securing her separation from the mother. This separation, unlike masculine separation is not based upon mastery and neither is it one based upon a quest for full autonomy. The girl is never fully separate from the mother. Instead 'the girl has the mother in some sense in her skin'. For Irigaray then, 'The Dance' provides a way in which to imagine a form of subjectivity which is very different from phallocentric representations. It describes subjectivity in terms of a set of relations which are not based upon a clear split between subject and object, or between interiority and exteriority.

Jacques Derrida also turns to the notion of 'Dance' as a means by which to describe a mode of non-phallocentric being. In response to a question about Emma Goldman's claim that 'if I can't dance, I don't want to be part of your revolution', Derrida suggests that perhaps Goldman has in mind 'a complete other history: a history of paradoxical laws and nondialectical discontinuities, a history of absolutely heterogenous pockets, irreducible particularities, unheard of and incalculable sexual differences . . . ' (1982: 442). Here, the concept of 'The Dance' provides a way of thinking beyond fixity, organisation and symmetry. However, unlike Irigaray, Derrida is keen to avoid any notion of what he calls the 'eternal Feminine'. Instead, he uses the metaphor of Dance as a way by which to get at a certain unfixing of truths about femininity. Dancing, he argues, 'is the displacement of women'. It is the destabilisation of sexual categories, including the category of 'woman' as an unproblematic basis for a revolutionary feminist politics. 'The Dance' opens the possibilities for disrupting established spaces, and for escaping those 'residences under surveillance'. It thus becomes a metaphor through which to imagine a certain disorganisation of subjectivity – a history not based on continuities, dualism and consensus but rather, upon dissymmetry, multiplicity and the innumerable.

In their different ways then, Irigaray and Derrida call upon the concept of 'The Dance' in their attempts at constructing alternative images of subjectivity and intersubjectivity; images which highlight the limitations of Humanist models. Although Irigaray has been repeatedly criticised for being essentialist, her work is perhaps most usefully considered, as it is by Braidotti, as a political fiction 'committed to the radical task of subverting conventional views and representations of human and especially female subjectivity' (1994, p. 3). Seen in these terms, 'The Dance' provides Irigaray with a means by which to formulate an alternative fiction about female subjectivity and along with Derrida's work, we can therefore situate hers as part of the growing philosophical move to produce alternative languages, images and figurations. In their aims at least, both Irigaray and Derrida share with Braidotti and Haraway the will to frame things 'otherwise'.

'The Dance' as it appears in such writing however, remains a concept. And the problem arises when the concept – an idealised version of 'The Dance' – comes to function as a catchall for all that is considered not rational or phallocentric. I therefore want to move from these philosophical abstractions and return to the embodied practices and situated accounts of female ravers. But I want to move whilst still holding onto the notion of producing alternative visions of the world. Although they use 'Dance' as a metaphor, the ways of being which both Irigaray and Derrida are getting at through such usage *do* resonate with the experiential claims of many raving women. That is to say, raving *is* often seen to involve a movement beyond fixity, coherence and rationality. It *is* commonly experienced as involving a dissolution of the division between self and other and between inner and outer. And it *is* repeatedly spoken about as affording alternative senses of being in the world. In short, it is experienced as a movement into somewhere 'else'; somewhere where subjectivity is stated 'otherwise'.

Elsewheres and otherwise

If raving can provide access to an 'elsewhere', then what does this 'elsewhere' look like? If it involves a rearticulation of the world, then how precisely is the world and subjectivity restated here?

The data discussed within the previous chapter suggests a radical reframing of the embodied subject within the rave event and here, I want to concentrate upon four particular aspects of this reframing – although these are not discussed individually. These are (1) notions of a movement of the individual self into a 'wider' body, (2) ideas about the inseparability of body from technology, (3) the celebration of a more fluid or 'autoerotic' sexuality and (4) the valorisation of 'madness'.

One of the most striking themes to emerge from these interviewees' accounts concerns the way in which subjectivity is restated in terms which do not reproduce traditional distinctions between self and other, between mind, body and spirit, between inner and outer or between physicality and technology. Instead, subjectivity is restated in the more ecological or relational terms of an ecstatic dancing body; a body which finds little place within the terms of Liberal Humanism's boundaried 'individual'. Indeed, almost all of these women describe raving as involving some kind of 'loss' of boundaries. Although, and as I argued in Chapter 1, it is dangerous to view such claims as straightforwardly indicative of a 'disappearance' of the self, they *do* suggest moments wherein the raving self is experienced as far more fluid – more 'in touch' with both itself and others, with music, with 'spirit' and so forth. The following claims are characteristic of this more 'fluid' or relational figuration:

> Although you're aware of yourself, you're in something bigger than yourself. And you can just spread out and – especially when you're on 'e' – your boundaries are just so stretched out, it isn't you any more, it's a whole thing. (Jane)

> It's really like you have spread out of your own individual boundaries and lose your limits. You feel like you really are bigger, or part of something bigger. (Amy)

The theme of losing oneself is thus accompanied in these accounts by the idea of an involvement within a wider, interconnected totality. Hence, the women speak of being 'bigger', or being part of 'something bigger'. Catherine articulates such sensations in terms of feeling part of a big, moving, coordinated animal, and Chris speaks about her first rave by stressing the synchronised connectedness between the different elements of the event:

> It's like being part of one big coordinated animal that just moves, and you're part of it. And it doesn't really matter if you personally stop dancing because even if you just stand there, it carries on and you still feel like you are part of it. (Catherine)

> I could really feel the thumping of the music going right through me and everything seemed to be in real harmony. Like the beat of the music and the strobes and the visuals. The crowd also looked really in-tune with it all. I was amazed at how everyone seemed to dance at the exact same pace. Like, everything was going as one. It all moved together. (Chris)

The sense of connectedness about which these women speak is not, then, limited simply to a feeling of being somehow 'in touch' with others. This is also about a connection to music, to technology, and to what several describe as something 'spiritual'. Miriam for example, tells me:

> Rave dancing is like putting you in contact with the spiritual world too. It's like meditation. It's not just the physicality of it, or the mental bliss. It's more than that. When you dance, you feel more whole. Yes, you're far more whole when you're dancing.

In similar ways Jane and Clare describe raving as a spiritual or a religious experience:

> It's a very spiritual experience really. You feel so in touch and so in contact with something bigger and more important. Like a vibe or an energy or something. And a lot of people think of that as a spiritual thing. (Jane)

> It's a spiritual experience almost. And that's not just in terms of the crowd euphoria aspect. It's also that it's an almost religious experience because you feel so good and so uplifted. Plus it's also like you've had something different revealed to you – you know, like a religious experience I guess. (Clare)

Like 'spirit', music is commonly seen as 'working through', or as inseparable from, the physical body. Miriam says:

> You're not separate from the music. The music *is* you. You are part of the music and there's no relationship even 'cause you're one.

This sense of connectedness does not simply apply to the loss of the individual self to a wider, interconnected 'body'. It also applies to understandings of mind/body relations. Typically, the women speak of experiencing an intense sense of oneness between their 'minds' and their 'bodies'. As Elaine puts this:

> You feel so whole. It's like . . . it's like you're really connected and sort of . . . kind of just whole.

And Catherine says:

> It's not just a body thing. It's not that your mind isn't there or that you're brain-dead. Absolutely not, because I always feel hyper-aware. Even a trance-like state isn't the same as being totally brain-dead because you can get so stimulated by things you see. And you can also get very emotional. So, it's not like you're a stone cold zombie. You feel, so it's very emotional. You don't actively 'think'. Like it's not like you have to force yourself to concentrate. You kind of relax into this feeling of wholeness.

The individual body is thus restated as just one component within a wider, interconnected circuit. The individual subject is decentred, and consciousness given over to the wider 'body' constructed in the process. The 'ecstatic moment' is thus, it seems, experienced as a release from monadic interiority – an outburst which represents less the loss of 'self' and more the absorption of the individual into a wider 'body'. As Clare puts this:

> You do just get so 'out of it' when . . . I mean you can just 'lose it' in all that movement. I don't know. It's all so connected and you become so much a *part* of it all.

As I pointed out earlier, this theme of the blurring of boundaries frequently extends to interviewee descriptions of sexuality and inter-bodily relations within an event. Commonly the women indicate modes of sexuality or eroticism which are 'blurred' or otherwise difficult to define. Statements like 'yes it's sexual. No, it's not' or 'no it's not sexual, but orgasmic' are common. And frequently, sexual attraction and erotic pleasure are seen to operate beyond sexual boundaries. In many cases, heterosexuality simply breaks down as a less definable, containable or even understandable formation comes into play:

It's not men or women. It's really just that sexual feeling for *every-one*. Yes, it is...well, sometimes. It *is* like a really intense attraction. (Catherine)

I kind of see it as a place where I can feel sexually about other people, but it doesn't actually go anywhere. It doesn't have to go anywhere 'cause that's it really. (Catherine)

Yes it is sexual I guess but not...it's not like...it is about *feeling* sexual but it's like feeling sexual for absolutely everybody, not just a single person or...like, you're not thinking about having sex with them but...No, you're not. But you feel so...it's like a sexual love for everyone. (Jane)

You've got something really unusual 'cause where normally, a woman directs her sexuality at a specific man and that specific man is a man of your choice, you just now flirt with...it's no one of your choice. You don't give a shit. You might be flirting with a woman as much as you're flirting with a man. You're just flirt-ing with the crowd. (Jane)

It's not sexual/physical like you have to touch someone. It's like a sexual feeling. It's more like a universal love rather than a single love for one other person. It's a sexual and loving feeling for every-one. (Teresa)

It's amazing. I don't think it's sexual like you're going to do some-thing with a...like you're going to get off with a bloke. But you *do* feel like sexy and you can be like 'cor, I feel so good and it *is* sex I reckon'. (Chris)

Well it's sexual kind of. No it's not sexual. It's different. (Amy)

It's not sexual but orgasmic. I wouldn't say it was sexual. It's different from being sexual. It's orgasmic in the sense of being very intense and reaching a peak. (Miriam)

In all of these instances, new forms of sexuality are being suggested. This is not about a sexual longing directed towards a specific or individual 'target', but about a far more dispersed and fragmented set of erotic energies which appear to be generated within the dance event. This new form of 'jouissance' has little to do with 'pick-up' or even with something outside the self (and this becomes particularly clear when several of the women use the term 'autoerotic'). The 'non-contact' and what Bradby calls 'non-reproductive' sexualities we find within the context of the contemporary dance event, clearly speak of a wider post-AIDS context. But they must also be situated within a post-feminist context, wherein heterosexual femininity is no longer so firmly centred around the heterosexual partnership. If traditional ideas about femininity's 'life-course' are being disturbed, then one thing that such a disturbance appears to be making way for, is the exploration upon the social dance floor, of sexualities which are less dictated by a normative heterosexual structure and which are, therefore, less about the situation of the female self in relation to a particular man or a general 'male gaze'.

Just like the images of the raver's blurred or ambiguous sexual sensations which emerge from these accounts, are the suggestions of 'mental' states which are equally blurred or confused. To go back to Elaine and Amy:

Rave is about going to the edge, which represents the edge between sanity and insanity. It's about losing it. (Elaine)

It's best for me when I feel like I can go completely mad – usually when I dance until I feel like I've expressed every single anxiety or pressure and it all comes out. It's like a safe space for going mad. (Amy)

Clearly and as I argued in Chapter 3, the role of the drug Ecstasy within the rave event cannot be undermined. But as I also suggested, this drug is best understood as part of rave as a mind/body/spirit/ technology assemblage which is 'rave'. 'E' is an important chemical component of this assemblage; a component which along with other material and discursive aspects such as music, visuals, the organisation of time, space and bodies, produces particular embodied experiences.

Nomadism, temporary connectedness and new female (be)longings

Above, I have touched upon some of the ways in which subjectivity is restated within the rave event. I now want to briefly indicate a final feature of the alternative 'world' seemingly opened up within rave. This concerns its very temporary nature. The 'elsewhere' into which the current interviewees describe moving is fleeting. In almost all of these accounts, what is being described is a 'world' which is known to be temporary, and within which relationships with (often anonymous) others appear to become all the more intense and important precisely because of their temporary nature. The descriptions of a 'universal love' for anonymous others which many of the women give, say a lot about a changed social world, a world within which traditional senses of 'community' and traditional ideas about female 'belonging' are breaking down. With the dissolution of the certainty promised by such structures, we find the emergence of what O'Connor (1997) (in Thomas (1997)) calls new 'communitas'. As I indicated earlier, O'Connor draws upon Lash and Urry (1994) in exploring the sense of 'communitas' generated within Set-Dancing groups, but her starting-points can be applied equally to the context of rave culture. With rave we very clearly have the kind of instant and ephemeral community which O'Connor writes about. The following statements illustrate very clearly the temporary – yet nevertheless very intense – relations and connections which can come about within the rave 'world':

> Yes, I feel totally connected to people in there. In like my favourite clubs, I do feel so close to the people. I recognise some of them, but mostly they're strangers even though I go regularly to that one place. You can feel extremely loving towards other people, it's true. (Amy)

> It is really lovely. It's quite spiritual really. It's just not ... 'cause you're not going to talk to any of these people again. It's such a different way of communicating. They don't know what you

do, what you're going to get up on Monday morning and do, you know. That's irrelevant. Who you came with is irrelevant. You can just smile at someone and that's it. You've made communication with them. (Jane)

I see these people and have really mad conversations with them about something. And you're never going to see them again, but you're never going to see everybody you meet again anyway. But the fact that you met them when you did is important because they've given you something of themselves and you've given them something of yourself. (Teresa)

I love it. It feels so warm. It's even ... sometimes it's even stronger than if you'd known them. But you *don't* know them. You probably won't ever see them again but it doesn't matter at all. That's not the point like ... like, it's not about making long-term buddies. It's there and it's then. That's it. (Clare)

I want to suggest that such descriptions resonate with Rosi Braidotti's image of the nomad, inasmuch as these women are talking about being within a community and a 'home' which is not based upon fixity and stability, but rather upon fleeting moments of intense interconnectedness with others. Braidotti writes:

Being a nomad, living in transition, does not mean that one cannot or is unwilling to create those necessarily stable and reassuring bases for identity that allow one to function in a community. Rather, nomadic consciousness consists in not taking any kind of identity as permanent. The nomad is only passing through: s/he makes the necessary connections that can help her/him to survive, but she never takes on fully the limits of one, national fixed identity. (1994, p. 33)

That the women understand the impermanence of the rave 'world' and also of the senses of self which emerge within this, is made very clear on several occasions. As Elaine puts it:

I know it passes and by ... it's sort of gone by a week later. It's still intense though and it still makes me want to keep going back to get back into it every now and again.

And Catherine says:

> You know it's going to fade. You know it'll all be gone in the
> morning. You'll pass that place a day or so later and . . . and you'll
> think I can't believe what was going on there on Saturday night. It
> is totally gone. Then the following week, it's there again and . . .
> and you're in it and it's all real again.

In writing of what he calls 'new sociations', Urry (1995) points out
that new kinds of groupings have come to replace the 'traditional'
community. These, he writes, provide:

> important sites whereby new kinds of social identity can be experi-
> mented with. They can empower people, they provide safe social
> spaces for identity-testing, and they provide a context for the
> learning of new skills. (1995, pp. 220–1)

Arguably, what the current interviewees appear to find within the rave
environment are the opportunities for exploring being and belonging
within a rapidly changing social world. This is a world within which
the traditional markers of adult femininity are becoming more and
more blurred, and within which many aspects of life (including relationships, employment and identities) are being recognised as
increasingly temporary.

Bad girls: other stories of femininity

'The most common argument about contemporary social dancing'
writes Sarah Thornton 'is that it empowers girls and women' (1995: 21).
Questions about whether social dance cultures are potentially empowering to women are central to many of the debates currently surrounding
rave. Such debates however, tend to focus primarily upon the organisational and production levels of rave culture, at the expense of
considering the enabling possibilities which this culture might open
up in terms of the generation of new fictions of femininity and for
attachments to such fictions. What I have attempted to show within
this chapter is that if we can speak of raving as being somehow
'empowering', then in large part, this is because we recognise that it
invites and encourages a suturing into alternative stories of female

being. Such stories are about an ecstatic 'insanity', an intense although temporary connectedness to others, a mode of being wherein the boundaries between physicality/machine, inner/outer, mind/body/ spirit, and self/other become so blurred as to no longer make much sense. Subjectivity is thus restated in ecological terms of an 'ecstatic' and interconnected assemblage.

What is striking about much club cultural commentary then, is its failure to recognise that what might be sexually 'empowering' about rave culture concerns its generation and provision of alternative fictions of femininity. For the present interviewees, one of rave's major appeals lies in its ability to offer them both new ways of experiencing themselves, and new ways of framing the world and intersubjectivity within this. These accounts speak of the constitution within the rave event of a particular mind/body/drug/spirit/technology assemblage which makes for alternative experiences of self.

I have suggested that the stories of these raving women resonate with those currently being told within certain realms of poststructuralist feminist philosophy. It is possible to see how, within rave, subjectivity and corporeality are being restated. The 'body' within rave is no longer simply the physical human body, or even a collection of these. Rather, this body includes technology (in the form of music, lighting and visuals), chemicals (in the form of drugs) and the 'spiritual'. This body is perhaps best understood therefore, in terms of what I have called a mind/body/spirit/technology assemblage. I have, in this chapter, concentrated primarily upon one aspect of this assemblage – embodied experiences. However, in highlighting the centrality of technology within this 'body', for example, I have also shown how this (like chemicals, music or architecture) is an important 'actor' within this constitution. Hence, although I am working with personal accounts, these are thought of as part of a wider machinery. It is then, possible to see within the constitution of the rave, an erosion of the limits between the corporeal and the technological and in this respect, it comes close to illustrating Haraway's reminder that 'not all actors have language' (1991). What Haraway is imagining here are the possibilities for human/machine relations which do not reproduce an active/passive split which prioritises language-bearing agents over non-human actors. What we can see within the particular mind/body spirit/technology assemblage constitutive of the rave event, is a positive female engagement with technology – an engagement which recognises the fluidity of borders between human and non-human.

Women within rave can be the 'bad girls' of which Donna Haraway writes. They can partake of the kind of nighttime and often illegal adventures which have traditionally been primarily the preserve of men. And they can engage themselves in an ecstatic unfixing or troubling of identity boundaries in the process. In some ways, it is *as-if* they were 'cyborgs'. Bradby, in writing about techno musical production, uses the same term but with specific reference to the relations between female voices, techno-music and sexuality. She sees within the particular female body/technology figuration which emerges from the use of female vocals within techno-music, the emergence of 'cyborgs' which, she says 'transgress the boundaries of Enlightenment equation of women with nature'. Such 'cyborgs' are, although in clearly different ways, equally evident at the level of musical consumption and in terms of what goes on upon the rave dance floor. Catherine, for example, says:

> You just can't stop sometimes. It's like you're being pushed to dance. I guess it's the drug as much as anything but it's the lights and the crowd too. The first time was really strange for me. Every-one around me looked like they were chopped up by strobes. I mean I could see heads here, arms there, all flashing up at differ-ent moments and it was actually a bit freaky. Then, when I got into it, it was amazing. You feel like you are a robot. (Catherine)

Rosi Braidotti argues that with her 'cyborg', Haraway is proposing a 'high-tech imaginary, where electronic circuits evoke new patterns of interconnectedness and affinity'. Such imaginary clearly comes through many of the accounts which I have discussed within this chapter. A centrally significant theme is one of interconnectedness, of the inseparability of the different components of the rave 'circuit'. This connectedness can be temporary, fleeting but it is still intense. And often it is seen to be based upon an 'energy' which cannot be reduced to or framed by language. Indeed, many emphasise the import-ance of rave as a non-verbal space which allows for the emergence of affinities not based upon language, but rather, upon ecstatic bodily relations. As Miriam puts it:

You didn't have to communicate with anyone verbally. It was very much a non-verbal communication. You'd just be dancing and you'd look round and look at someone in the eyes and you knew that that person was experiencing exactly the same as you were experiencing and there was a direct sort of bond with that person.

This celebration of an unspoken interconnectedness over the verbal partly explains why rave culture has been so very hard to understand as a 'political' one. Compared with previous youth movements founded upon 'statement'-making, it looks extremely empty. If it has attempted to 'politicise' itself, rave has done this partly as a defence of the 'freedom to party'. Within this space, alternative kinds of inter-connections, affinities and relationships are made possible. These may be fleeting or temporary, but this in no way undermines their intensity.

To reiterate, above all else, if rave and club cultures are 'empowering' women, then they do so by providing the material and discursive conditions for the explorations of different embodiments of femininity. In Urry's terms, they provide the conditions within which new social identities can be explored, and within which new skills can be learnt. Living with the temporary, coping with confusion and dealing with 'madness' – these are some of the skills seemingly being explored within contemporary rave cultures.

5
Peak Practices: the Production and Regulation of Ecstatic Bodies

In the previous two chapters, I concentrated upon the experiential accounts which came out of the series of interviews I conducted with a group of raving women. In Chapter 3, I highlighted the specific role which rave plays within these different women's lives, and in the last chapter, I explored what these accounts might be saying more generally about contemporary reframings of sexed subjectivity-in-context. Here, I focused on the make-up of the alternative 'world' into which many claim to 'trip' when raving, and on the kinds of subjectivities which emerge within this 'world'. A central aim of both of these chapters was to argue that if raving can be seen as in any way 'empowering' these women, then this is centrally because it appears to enable them to tell and live very different fictions of femininity – fictions which I have suggested are in some ways, perhaps, more suited to a changing social world.

In the present chapter, I want to add a further dimension to this ongoing analysis, by looking to the 'work' which goes into producing a state which comes to be experienced as one of 'pure freedom' (Sally). The aim is simple. I want to challenge any oversimplistic reading of raving as a somehow *essentially* or *basically* liberating practice. It would be easy to approach these interviewees' accounts and present a straightforwardly celebratory story about a contemporary club-world filled with 'mad', 'liberated', 'post-feminist' women who radically challenge the traditional equation of women with sobriety, enclosure and 'safety'. Of course, in part, this is precisely what I have attempted to argue. But this is not the whole story. If these women are attaching to alternative stories of femininity, then this attachment clearly takes a certain amount of work. To put this another way, an effective sutur-ing into these stories requires that a particular manner of textual engagement be adopted. And here, I want to illustrate some of the operations involved in such an adoption. These women then, may well feel freed-up from their situation in relation to more traditional stories of femininity (a loosening up which clearly carries with it a number of enabling possibilities) but this 'freedom' is obviously not about returning to some kind of essential, pre-social or otherwise more basic core. And neither is it about a complete escape from regu-lation. There is no such thing as a purely unregulated self. The women may well trip into a 'mad' and adventurous 'elsewhere' wherein subjectivity is stated otherwise, but the journeys to these elsewheres are not always so smooth and the routes into them are not always so easy to find. Reaching their destination often involves for these women, struggle against a number of potential obstacles. This is not then, about an escape from regulation. On the contrary, it is about regulating the self as a *different* kind of one, or about bringing a very *different* self into being.

As has historically been the case in interpreting youth cultures, a familiar association between the practices of rave and notions of 'freedom' has emerged. Since its beginnings in the late 1980s, British rave culture has thrown up its own version of what this 'freedom' entails and looks like. This is about 'going mental', 'losing it' and get-ting 'out of it'. Corresponding to this particular version of 'freedom' has been the development of what, drawing upon Michel Foucault (1988), we might call certain 'technologies of the self' which function in the pursuit and maintenance of a particular sought-after state of being. As Foucault explains:

> Technologies of the self... permit individuals to effect by their own means or with the help of others a number of operations on their bodies and souls, thought, conduct and way of being, so as to transform themselves in order to attain a certain state of happi-ness, purity, wisdom, perfection or immortality. (1988, p. 18)

Too often, critics ignore the fact that raving might involve such operations on the self. Instead, it is commonly implied that raving *simply* transforms the socialised self into a freer, less regulated, state of being – a transformation which reveals a more basic human core beneath or behind its socialised exterior. Somehow, the use of drugs, the effects of music, the practice of communal social dance and the collective nature of rave events are seen to dissolve this exterior, leaving participants in a somehow more 'natural' state. Some academic readings of this culture therefore make claim to ravers' pre-Oedipal nature of being (Reitveld, 1994), whilst others, invoke the primitivist language of shamanism and tribalism (Hamment, 1995). Tim Jordan (from Thomas, 1997) sees rave constituting a form of 'unregulated' space reminiscent of Hakim Bey's 'Temporary Autonomous Zone' (TAZ) and Richard Sutcliffe (1996) also emphasises autonomy, in arguing that rave is about free corporeal expression in relation to music. Sutcliffe attributes individual experiences of autonomy to the collective autonomy of rave organisation which he likens to Deleuze and Guattari's notion of a 'war machine', that is rhizomatic in form and resistant to fixture. And as I indicated earlier, the language of Deleuze and Guattari is also called upon by Jordan who reads rave as a 'Body without Organs' (BwO) and who suggests that rave dance-floor movement is best captured through the concept of Lines of Flight.

Very general arguments such as the above are however, often difficult to support empirically. Sutcliffe for instance, makes an automatic connection between practices that may fall outside state bureaucratic control (an argument which is itself questionable) and a 'free' form of subjectivity. Equally dubious is the argument (as this appears within Redhead's 'Rave Off') that rave is a culture of 'disappearance' which somehow resists meaning, and which cannot therefore be classified and appropriated by the academy. Ravers themselves, however, – and despite the fact that they too often celebrate the 'freedom' they find within an event – very often indicate that a quite rigorous self-regulation, monitoring and management is an integral part of raving. And this is what I shall concentrate upon shortly.

Where rave culture is likened to a TAZ or to a BWO, with the implication that it is somehow less rule-bound and hierarchically structured than other forms of collective organisation, ravers are commonly read as embodiments of 'freedom'. Their subjective 'freedom' is assumed to stem from the absence of classificatory devices and masterful gazes which apparently characterise other more 'coherent' forms of subjectivity. As I indicated earlier, Reitveld for example, writes that raving involves an 'undoing of the constructed self', and Jordan argues that:

> In these vast celebrations usually called raves, participants gradually lose subjective belief in their self and merge into a collective body whose nature is best captured by Deleuze and Guattari's concept of the Body without Organs. (1995, p. 125)

Whilst I clearly do not deny the very genuine senses of 'freedom' which can be involved in raving, nor the feeling which the raver can experience of having lost 'coherence', 'rationality' or 'sanity', I also believe that a more cogent interrogation of the precise nature of this perceived 'freedom' is overdue. As my previous discussions have suggested, raving can equally (and in my view, more accurately) be understood as enabling the transformation of the self into something *different*, rather than as simply involving some kind of 'disappearance' of the self. Selves are 'done' as much as they are 'undone' within rave. Ravers can very clearly be seen to carry out certain operations upon their bodies, souls, thought and being in order to achieve a sought-after state of ecstatic 'freedom'.

In order to explore in more detail some of the operations involved in the production and maintenance of the 'peak' state which many seek out within the rave event, I want to turn to one particular group interview which I conducted with Sally and Jean, two 19-year-old ravers. I want to focus upon this interview because aside from what it says about the excitement and 'freedom' which both of the women associate with raving, it also indicates that a certain anxiety or struggle is involved in reaching the experiential state being sought within the rave event. In short, although – and like many of the other interviewees – Sally and Jean claim that rave is central to their lives, that it is something they cannot imagine wanting to stop and that it brings with it an incomparable sense of 'liberation', as their accounts unfold, it becomes obvious that in order to reach a 'peak' within an event, a certain amount of hard 'work' needs to be undertaken. The music, the drugs, the venue, the crowd and the atmosphere must all be 'right'. Certain elements must be avoided in striving towards a 'peak', and certain steps need to be taken in the maintenance of this 'peak'. Simply walking through the door of a rave event, or simply 'popping' a particular pill, in no way guarantees access to the experiential world into which these women want to trip. The raving state of ecstatic 'freedom' must be actively brought into being and maintained – and frequently this involves struggle.

Highlighting, as I do briefly within this chapter, the work involved in the production of an 'ecstatic', 'free' or 'peak' state is not however, about denying or undermining the very real pleasures and senses of liberation and autonomy which women such as Sally and Jean get from raving. It is simply about showing how such a state is brought into being. To argue that an experiential moment of 'freedom' might be produced whilst being monitored and otherwise constructed is not to argue that it is not 'real'. In short, just because raving can pro-vide important senses of 'freedom' from certain wider day-to-day regulatory practices (including perhaps, the self-practices involved in, say, going to college, caring for a child, working or negotiating a relationship) and equally important senses of liberation from more traditional fictions of femininity (including stories about 'good girls indoors'), this does not mean that it constitutes an essentially unregulated space. To reiterate, there is no such thing as an entirely unregulated space or an essentially unregulated subject, and even the (very real) experience of 'freedom' can be shown to involve its own regulatory and self-governmental mechanisms. This is a frequently overlooked issue within most club cultural commentary. Commonly, the rave event is talked about as though this existed in some kind of post-apocalyptic 'beyond' within which both meaning and the sub-ject are dead. Here, little or no consideration is given to the various operations which work towards the production of what may come to be experienced as a state of meaninglessness, freedom or 'undone' selfhood and the work which goes into maintaining such a state. Instead, the impression is given that the raver finds or enters this state of 'freedom' simply, or automatically, as a result of being within the rave environment. What follows is an attempt to upset such oversimplicity.

But although my focus here is upon the work, struggle or energy which these women put into reaching the 'peak' they seek I also want to stress that Sally and Jean (whose account I am focusing on) were two of the most animated and excited interviewees with whom I worked. Both get from raving some of their happiest moments and both agree that within their lives more broadly, raving is almost as important to them as is motherhood. So, and to reiterate, although

I am concentrating upon some of their work, struggles and anxieties, this is not about denying, undermining or even questioning the importance and centrality of rave within their lives. To reiterate, it is simply about showing how such states of 'freedom' are produced, and also about illustrating the great lengths to which the women will go in order to hold onto the spaces and practices which enable them to produce and experience such states.

The Constitution of a Peak Moment

Writing over a decade ago, Simon Reynolds (in McRobbie, 1989) makes the following observation:

> Our culture has long since ceased to demand deferment of grat-
> ification or sublimation of energy: it insists on enjoyment, incites
> us to develop our capacity for pleasure. 'Youth' – because coter-
> minous with sex, style, hedonism, fitness – has become the supreme
> value in society, almost the definition of health. Our economy
> demands an intense and versatile desire on the part of consumers:
> growth depends on a high turnover not just of commodities and
> fashions, but increasingly a gamut of off-the-peg self-expression
> (therapies, self-improvement, cultural experiences) ... Pop has always
> been bodymusic, but the body is now the prime locus of power's
> operation, where power solicits us. Being a success in life involves
> a maximisation of your body's potential for health and pleasure
> (aerobics, sexology, nutrition, massage, touch-therapy, TM and so
> on) (1989, p. 246).

If Reynolds sees, within the popular cultural practices of the mid-
eighties, a growing incitement to the heightening of bodily pleasures, then rave can be seen to have taken this to an extreme in the
1990s. As I have argued elsewhere, within the rave, it is the individual mind/body which is (often relentlessly) 'worked on' in the
pursuit of the 'peak' or 'limit' experience (Pini, 1997a). The accounts
given by Sally and Jean are particularly interesting, because these
make so obvious some of the work, management, regulation and
monitoring which goes into the production of a moment which
comes to be experienced as one of 'pure freedom' or what Jean calls
'pure self-expression'. Indeed, both women state explicitly, that they

have to 'work' in order to achieve and maintain the sought-after ecstatic state. 'You *do* have to work for it', Jean tells me. This 'work' includes keeping a constant check on the self and its surroundings for potential disturbances to the ecstatic state. As the following extracts indicate, paranoia, sickness, 'attitude', the 'wrong' music, the 'wrong' look or word from a fellow raver, the 'wrong' venue, the 'wrong' drugs and even the 'wrong' clothes (Jean's high-heeled boots), all pose threats to the achievement and maintenance of this state.

(i) On the management and regulation of energy, pain and drugs

J: And 'cause I do so many pills, I just use all my energy and stop dancing at about four and then if I can, I try . . . I *do* try to pace it and do another one or two but you know, it doesn't always work.

J: I used to do eight Speed pills. I got up to eight, doing eight. But that *did* make me paranoid. I couldn't go down the town on my own, 'cause I felt stupid and paranoid. So, I've gone lower and that's made me better actually. So, I was doing five. I normally take with me five. You learn what you need.

S: I got a lot of throat problems and with Speed you just get all the dry throat and that, so I got to make sure I drink and that 'cause the throat can kill me sometimes. Next day, I can't speak.

S: I sometimes have to just run through the crowd. Like you pretend to cough like . . .

J: But *really*, you're vomiting aren't you?

S: Yeah.

J: It *can* make you really sick.

J: I get really bad cramp, don't I?

S: Yeah.

J: It's like a knife stuck in your leg. I feel really bad and it is *so* bad sometimes. I have to sit, and *then* I ain't sure if I'll be able to get up.

S: Sometimes, I'll take it slow for . . . Like you don't go mad for the first few hours. You kind of save yourself else you'd be finished when other people are coming up.

J: Yeah, like that one I was saying – with the boots and I realise right, it's the long boots with heels that's making me not dance and like I couldn't dance right, and that's what did it. Not like being able to dance properly and I'm like 'uh' and I'm *not* having a good time. And it's only an hour and I'm wanting to go.

(ii) Avoiding 'bad attitude' and paranoia

S: You get the attitude, from the boys and the girls. But it does happen.

J: Yeah, you just got to try and ignore it...just like, they're just trying to do your head in, so you just got to ignore it. It...people sometimes want to do your head in, so you got to just blank it.

S: Yeah, they just want to make you paranoid

J: Well, it's like if you're paranoid, you just feel that everybody's looking at you. If it's paranoid when I stop dancing, I still feel that everybody's looking at me. Like at *this* one, I'd been trying to get into it to [DJ's set] after the 'Happy' music had been on, and we was in the centre kind of thing, at the front but in the centre of the crowd. And I *tried* and I *pushed*, but I couldn't do it again. After standing there for a while, I started getting looks. I mean, I weren't fucked-up. I was fine at that point – until people started looking. When they was looking at me as if to say 'cor mate, she's fucked-up.' But I *wasn't*. I was just standing there. But *'cause* these people kept looking at me like I was, it started making me think 'uh, mate'. And then I started going all spacey on my feet and that – where you can't like, stand.

J: That was paranoia. This one bloke walked past and went 'you alright?' And I went 'yeah, yeah. I've *just* come down. That's all.' Did my head in. I just feel like everybody's looking at me and half the time, they probably *are* 'cause I'm feeling like that. I'm making a look on my face maybe, you know. I don't know. I hate it. I *hate* that feeling. I feel like I *have* to get out.

Throughout their accounts, and as the above statements demonstrate 'peaking' or 'rushing' take a certain amount of organisation, management and even hard work. The women 'work' to dance. They 'work' to get along with others. And they 'work' to 'rush'. Below for example, Jean describes having to 'push it' in order to 'peak' on her drugs:

And we tried to get some Speed but we couldn't get none, so we got like six E's. Three E's each. And like it was only because you couldn't get any Speed-pills – so it was a bit of a risk. I didn't do them all at once, but as I was doing them, I wasn't coming-up on them, you know. I find that on a lot of E's though. To begin with, you have got to push it. And then like, I'd done the 3 E's and was feeling nothing and I thought fucking hell, I've just borrowed all this money to come up to London and I'm sitting down and I've got to push this. So I was like, *push it. Push it.*

Both Sally and Jean thus give the impression that the 'peak' or 'ecstatic' moment is achieved 'against the odds' so to speak, or against a backdrop of a whole host of possible obstacles. It is not just the achievement but also the maintenance of the 'peak' state, which requires work. The 'wrong' music, the 'wrong' attitude, the 'wrong' look and so on, all have the potential to bring the raver 'down'. All of these things carry the power to radically disturb how the raver wants to experience and understand herself within an event.

(iii) Negotiating good and bad gazes

If, as I argued earlier, many of the present interviewees are able to attach, through raving, to alternative fictions of femininity, then Sally and Jean's accounts suggest that a number of potentially disturbing factors threaten their embodiment of such fictions. Significantly, the emphasis which the women place upon particular (either 'good' or 'bad') gazes suggests that the sought-after 'ecstatic' state is in some respects, about a desire to be seen or positioned in a particular way. It is as if the 'wrong' look or gaze from someone (as exemplified, by the staring crowd, or the gaze of the 'attitudie' for instance) threatens to bring into question the particular image of self which the raver wants to entertain. Jean says, in continuing her description of feeling paranoid when she is not dancing within an event:

Yeah, like I can't ... does my head in when you get those like attitudes like staring at you. And you know. It's like *going* to bring you down. You know, I'm like 'cor mate, I'm just standing here, you know. Nothing'. Like that's it, but it's bringing me down.

Jean's concerns about being stared or looked at within an event suggest the extent to which the pleasures of raving are in some ways tied up for the women with having others see and frame them within a particular desired light – or in other words, having others confirm a particular vision of the self. Their pleasures and displeasures do appear to be partly informed by the extent to which other ravers confirm or contradict how they want to see themselves when raving. If certain gazes bring them 'down', then others serve to intensify their 'rush'. As Jean puts it for instance, having a 'horny man' look at her, makes her 'whoosh'. What is clear from this account therefore, is the extent to which the pleasures of raving can be very closely tied into the pleasures of being able to entertain a particular view of the self. Both women stress that within a rave, one performs a very different type of self. This self has to be brought into being and maintained. It is fragile, and something like the 'wrong' look from a fellow raver, can radically threaten it. The conditions for performing a particular self must, then, be in place and the subjectifying 'gazes' must be correct. This is clearly not about an undoing or disappearance of the self, but about bringing into being a particular and different kind of self.

(iv) Dodging constraints and pressures

Sally and Jean thus make it clear how much work they put into achieving and maintaining a sought-after state *within* an event. But, the organisation and management do not stop here. The account also highlights just how much work they have to do before and after an event in order that they can stake out the time and the 'right' to rave in the first place. Child-care is obviously one consideration which figures highly in both of their accounts. Pressures from their casual boyfriends also require a certain management. Jean, for example tells me that her boyfriend (even though he lives with another of his regular sexual partners) will often not 'let' her rave if he is not with her: 'I couldn't say you know, "me and Sally want to go to *Desire*." No, I couldn't say "me and Sally want to go to *Desire*", and he'd say "OK. No way."'

Jean has therefore devised certain strategies for going out to raves without her boyfriend discovering this (usually she lies to him and claims to be going to her mother's). She also describes, on several occasions, how she deliberately 'loses' him when they go to raves together. She explains, for instance:

> I mean, say, if I am talking to a geezer, I've always got that constant fear of Peter wandering by and seeing me. 'Cause he is *so* jealous.

I have to be careful. So what I tend to do is dance until I come-down. I've always got people coming up to me saying 'Pete's looking for you.' I'm 'yeah, yeah. Alright. I mean don't tell him you've seen me' kind of thing. Then, when I come-down, I go find him.

Just as the women describe doing things which they do not want their boyfriends to see, they also describe having to manage their weekends in order that their children do not see them as ravers. Their weekends therefore have to be quite strictly organised, allowing them both 'coming up' time (the hours they spend getting ready and getting high before going out) and 'come-down' time (usually on Sundays when they simply lie around recovering):

> J: You *know* you're going to have a come-down and you know it's going to be bad.
> S: We know what happens after every rave, don't we?
> J: Yeah. You're going to come down.
> J: Absolutely. I wouldn't be on drugs around them 'cause, nah. For a start I couldn't have [her son] back on like, a come-down. I wouldn't have him back because . . . 'mum can I have this. Can I have that.' And I would lose my patience. I couldn't do it.
> S: Yeah, it's not fair on them.
> J: No, 'cause they're at that early age now. I wouldn't like them to see me like that. They've got to have all your attention anyway, init? So I mean he's down my mum's. They like that anyway, so. . . .
> S: Basically, you ain't fit enough afterwards.
> J: No. It's alright you know. My mum has him for a couple of days so when I get him back, my come-down's gone.
> S: Yeah, when I go raving, it's always on a Saturday night and I don't get her [daughter] back until the Monday. She goes to her dad's. Nah, you know what the weekend is, and Sunday's out.
> J: Yeah, you got to make sure that the kids ain't around on the Saturday night or the Sunday. I wouldn't let him see me like if we're speeding before we leave. Not speeding or come-down. I don't want him seeing me like that. I'm very different from normal and it would be weird for him.

Alongside their organisation of childcare and the energy which they put into finding ways around their boyfriends' attempts to stop them raving, Sally and Jean also have to do a certain amount of financial organisation in order to rave. As they explain it:

> J: You do make sacrifices. Ticket's twenty-five pounds.
> S: And petrol's another thing.
> J: And pills. I get my pills for four pounds, so that's four, eight, twelve, sixteen, twenty pounds. And if you do half an 'E', twenty-five pounds. So fifty or sixty pounds. But then, you got your outfit as well, if you're going to get an outfit, but I do – every time. So that's about say eighty pounds say. You see, I work my money out all the time. All the time, I work my money out for the weeks coming ahead and then you know when you start saving, when you can buy your ticket out of one week, and start paying for your drugs.

(v) The classification, regulation and 'knowledge' of experience

If raving for Sally and Jean can be seen to involve a certain management, then such management is shown to be made possible partly because of the clear and heavy classification of a range of features. In order to manage, the women must *know* what they are dealing with. And within their account, everything from people, to towns, to drugs, to music are classified and known accordingly. Distinctions are made between 'happy ravers' and 'attitudies'; between 'Speed' towns and 'E' towns; between 'rushy Es', 'mellow Es' and 'smacky Es'; between 'Happy house music', 'Jungle' and 'Garage'; between 'horny men' and 'ugly men'; between 'Speed-heads' and 'E-heads', and between a 'nice look' from someone and a 'wrong look' from someone. Experiential states are similarly classified. The raver can be 'coming up', 'coming down', 'rushing', 'handling it', 'losing it' and so forth. Such terms – rather than being mere descriptions – are very obviously learnt. Indeed, on several occasions, it becomes clear that these women have come to learn what it is that they are actually experiencing. For example, a knowledge of drug-effects develops which clearly constructs as much as it describes these very effects. This becomes clear when, on several occasions, the women talk about having felt uncertain about how they were feeling at a particular time. This uncertainty is then overcome once the women 'know' what they are supposed to expect. In the following extract for example, Jean describes feeling bad after having taken a pill, until she comes to 'know' that this is *in fact*, good:

> And I thought I was losing it. Yeah, that's why. I hadn't been raving for two years and I went for my birthday to 'World Dance'. I was only in there about an hour and a half 'cause I walked in ... First of all, the beat was different. It was faster, and instead of walking into the rave and thinking 'cor, yeah', I thought 'shit'. I started coming up on the 'E' and it was a totally different feeling to the Speed, see. So I wasn't expecting all that ... I didn't like it you know. And I went outside and I was right off my head, and I thought I was losing it. But now I *know* that it was just a good 'E' you know.

Later on in the interview, Jean tells a similar story. Again, she describes feeling unsure about whether or not she is 'up' and how she comes to realise that rather than having taken 'dud' pills, she has actually taken pills which are too strong: 'And it was just that it was good stuff but I didn't realise. I thought it just didn't work.'

Just as they have come to 'know' drug-effects, Sally and Jean have also come to know drug states and stages within both themselves and within each other. The development of this kind of knowledge of drugs, stages and states is thus shown to be an integral part of raving. Indeed, both of the women indicate that they have come to learn the precise chemical 'ingredients' best suited to them as ravers. In the light of this knowledge, a clear governing of drug-intake and a related set of rules surrounding this intake develops:

> J: With Speed, you know what you're getting. That's right. You get ... I'm an active person anyway so I love Speed. With E's you never know if you're going to get a Smacky one. But if you're having half an E or an E with all the Speed you've got, then you're not going to get Smacked-out on that – with that amount of Speed, you know. So it just makes you even better.
> J: At first like you never ... never do a whole E. Not at first. My first E was a whole one and it was a Dove, so I'd say don't do a whole E ...
> S: No ...
> J: I'd even do it in quarters I think ...

S: Yeah, when you're starting off right . . .

J: Yeah, at first when you've never done it before.

Corresponding to such knowledge about drugs, a clear set of risk-assessment strategies develops. Throughout the interview, the women repeatedly detail the set of 'guidelines' which seem to govern their drug-taking practices:

J: You know you're taking a risk.

S: You take a risk.

J: If you're gonna do E's you drink a lot of water and then you're not going to drop dead of dehydration.

S: Nah, don't . . . like you mustn't let yourself get too hot.

J: Yeah, you got to stop for breaks 'cause it can be bad . . .

S: Yeah.

J: Like, cool off for a bit is what you . . . don't keep going if . . .

S: Like, you got to have a break.

Freedom reconsidered

In this chapter, I have briefly tried to show how what is commonly thought of as a moment of 'freedom' and 'pure self-expression' is far more complex than is usually acknowledged by academic commentators and ravers alike. I have indicated how for Sally and Jean, their 'free' state is in actuality one that is, in many respects, carefully managed, regulated, monitored and otherwise produced. Far from being about the 'loss' or 'undoing' of the self, rave actually involves the production of a particular state, or the bringing into being of a particular 'ecstatic' self. And this production can very clearly be seen to involve a certain amount of quite rigorous work and organisation.

But and importantly, just because the Ecstatic state is shown to be produced, this does not mean that it is not 'real' in its effects, important in terms of its significance within a wider life context, or that it is not genuinely and uniquely pleasurable. Sally and Jean may well face many constraints or problems relating to finances, health and relationships when it comes to raving, but still they refuse to give this up. Despite the constraints, pressures and obstacles they face, rave remains fundamentally important to their lives. Indeed, it is impossible to reproduce in writing quite how excited and animated the women become when speaking about rave. At one point, they say:

> J: You get the withdrawal symptoms if it's been too long, don't you? It's like 'got to go raving'. As soon as you got all your friends up here, and you got your tunes on and that, you start talking about it and getting hyped and you really want to be there again, don't you?
>
> S: Yeah, like a week beforehand, you're building yourself up for it. You got your music on. Especially the day – the day before. The day itself.
>
> J: Like doing the housework ain't it, with music full-blast. You got, got to go . . .
>
> S: It makes you feel so good afterwards, once you've been to a rave. You've got everything out of your system and then a while passes and you think, I've got to go to rave.
>
> J: The only thing is where you've waited so long for that night to come, the next day, you're out in the car and you think, God, it's over. You've got to go through all the waiting again. It's always the same.

This analysis is in no way intended therefore, as a way of denying what women like Sally and Jean get from raving. It is not about undermining the real senses of 'liberation' which the rave offers them. And neither is it about contradicting my earlier arguments. Like all of the other interviewees, Sally and Jean find within rave the possibilities for embodying very different fictions of femininity from those which they can live as mothers, girlfriends or as young, unemployed women. These different fictions may well appear fragile. They may well be temporary and they may well require that a particular manner of textual engagement be adopted in order that a sought-after state be achieved – an adoption which may sometimes involve work and struggle. But none of this makes attachments to these alternative fictions any less meaningful.

Conclusions: 'Losing It': Dance Cultures and New Modes of Femininity

That the significance of being a woman is currently undergoing some important changes is indisputable. Although nobody is suggesting that changes to femininity are happening uniformly, or denying that the speed and form of their development are bound to reflect social divisions based upon race, education and social class for example, it is nevertheless clear that as we enter a new millennium, we do so leaving behind us many of the values, attitudes and assumptions which have long underpinned dominant ideas about femininity's 'rightful' place and its 'appropriate' life-course. Familiar constructions of femininity are being quite rapidly eroded as increasingly, women invest more and more time, energy and desire outside the domestic and familial realms, outside the heterosexual partnership, and in short, outside those 'happy-ever-after' narratives of romantic closure.

Of course, feminism has been central in bringing about such changes. Although there are clearly problems with imagining that this is *one* thing, or that this one thing has informed all women in the same way, its many effects are undeniable. As Angela McRobbie rightly argues:

> Despite the hostility of the tabloid press, feminism has had a dramatic impact on almost every level of social life in Britain. It has made issues around sexual equality part of the political agenda in both the private sphere of the home and in domestic relations, and in the more public world of work. Likewise, institutions themselves (particularly in education) have been alerted to the question of women and young women as economic agents, participating in

189

the economy for the greater part of their lives. Altogether this kind of heightened activity around questions of gender has radically undermined what might be described as the old domestic settlement which tied women (and young women's futures) primarily to the family and to low-paid or part-time work.

In addressing changes to femininity, Helen Wilkinson writes of a 'Genderquake', whilst McRobbie (although acknowledging the problems with such generalisations) identifies a deep shift in the consciousness of women from different generations, different parts of the country and different social classes. What she calls a 'semi-structure' of feminist feeling is now part of what it means to be a woman. However we choose to speak of it, it is obvious that in so many important ways, traditional fictions of femininity are becoming less and less effective in inviting women to identify. If we think of female identity as arising from a process whereby the subject is, as Hall puts it, 'sutured into' a story, then the story is changing, or at very least it is being quite radically rewritten. In place, we are witnessing the emergence of what are in many respects, very new and unfamiliar fictions of femininity.

Club Cultures and Female Subjectivity has been a study of how such changes are manifest in relation to women's accounts of their contemporary club cultural practice. And it has been such a study precisely because I consider club cultures to be particularly fruitful sites for an exploration of emerging fictions of femininity. Not everyone would agree, and it could of course be argued that it would have been possible to ask more or less the same questions which I have posed within this work, in relation to a completely different cultural practice. And it is true that in some ways at least, this need not necessarily have been an analysis of dance cultures. The labour market, the education system, the family, the world of women's magazines or the realm of popular (literary and cinematic) fiction, would undoubtedly have all provided rich sites for an analysis of the new discourses coming to cohere around femininity. And it is likely that many of the same themes upon which I have focused within this work, would have emerged. Speaking a language of 'freedoms', voicing a reluctance to remain 'enclosed' within the home, challenging 'predatory' (or otherwise oppressive) modes of masculinity, stressing autonomy and emphasizing self-pleasure are arguably all aspects which could have emerged from a study of femininity in relation to something quite different.

But it really is only partly true that this could have been a study of women's involvements within a different cultural practice. Like Barbara Bradby, I believe that contemporary club cultures are particularly important sites for the articulation of new forms of sexed subjectivity. Precisely because social dance spaces are physically quite distinct from the day-to-day worlds of work, school, home and responsibility; precisely because social dance *is* a night-time practice and hence, exercised in a time which is also removed from the day-to-day; precisely because dance is a leisure activity, and precisely because on the social dance floor different 'worlds', different forms of sexuality, different senses of 'home' and different kinds of 'communities' can be brought into being, club cultures are especially significant places for the working out of new ideas and ways of being. These new 'homes' or communities, are as Urry (1995) points out, spaces wherein a certain identity-testing and skill-learning can take place. One of the central issues which I have concentrated upon within this study, is how with the breakdown of traditional fictions of femininity, club cultures can come to constitute important sites for an exploration and testing of alternatives.

However, it is not just because dance clubs *in general* promise a certain removal from the day-to-day, that they come – for the women interviewed here – to feel like alternative spaces. The present has been a study specifically of rave and post-rave dance cultures. Precisely because these are seen to be relatively 'safe' and relatively free of 'predatory' male behaviour, precisely because raving is seen to be centrally about dance rather than sexual pick-up, and precisely because women feel able to get 'out of it', 'go mental' or 'lose it' without putting themselves at risk, these cultures are different from traditional nightclub cultures. No longer is the heterosexual 'pick-up' such a central point. No longer, is 'adventure' a primarily male preserve. No longer is 'getting out of it' seen to conflict with 'proper' femininity. No longer are women expected or thought to be simply uninterested in drugs, 'madness' or in the intense self-absorption which can come from raving. With rave, different conditions are in place – conditions which allow for the fabrication, embodiment and exploration of very different fictions of femininity. These are fictions where an insistence upon the 'right' to adventure, a valorisation of 'madness' and a celebration of 'autoeroticism' are central. And these are fictions which are fundamentally challenging to what McRobbie calls the 'old domestic settlement'.

Although I have spoken about the fictions of femininity being generated within rave culture as somehow different from those which surround us within a broader cultural sphere, these are obviously not in any way neatly separable from their wider context. Such fictions always reference their broader situation. If raving women 'make statements' then these are always located, context-specific statements. They speak of and to, a broader cultural condition. In *Subculture: the Meaning of Style*, Dick Hebdige surveys the different ways in which subcultural theorists have attempted to understand the relations between parent-cultures and subcultures. Although the split which such terms suggest are not particularly useful here (because dance cultures hardly constitute 'subcultures' and because very often, ravers are hardly 'youths') maintaining a sense of the difference between the 'day-to-day' world and the 'world' of clubs and raves is necessary. For all of the reasons which I have spoken about within this work, clubs and raves *are* often experienced and understood as kinds of 'elsewheres'. So although the notion of the 'parent' and the 'subculture' may not be of much use to us here, an idea of the 'here' and the 'elsewhere' is. We can view this 'elsewhere' as a kind of gap, or as a space which is somehow removed from the everyday and within which some kind of reflection, assessment, exploration, negotiation and feedback is made possible. Part of this exploration appears to involve the kind of magical resolution of contradictions which Hebdige refers to in reviewing Phil Cohen's work on youth subcultures. For Cohen, the subculture works as a space within which the tensions and contradictions involved in the parent culture are symbolically worked out. The same might easily be said about femininity and contemporary dance cultures. At a time when femininity – its meanings, identity and life-course – is undergoing a quite radical loosening up, when traditional forms of 'community' are quite rapidly eroding, when a sense of impermanence increasingly comes to mark relationships and work, instant and ephemeral dance-cultural 'worlds' are being generated; worlds within which 'madness', 'autonomy' and self-absorption can coexist alongside senses of absolute unity and complete connectedness. Within this world 'losing it' is made safe. Whether this means the loss of femininity's traditional landmarks, or the loss of 'sanity' and 'head' which can come from raving, loss is somehow made manageable. Hence – although it is clearly not the *whole* story – in part, it does seem to be the case that the club cultural space can come to constitute a kind of new page or an empty plane upon which new fictions can be written, new landmarks can be built or in Susan McClary's terms, new experiential worlds can be articulated. It is useful then, to think of the contemporary social dance event as involving this kind of work-in-process. The construction of new landmarks of femininity is part of this work. But, and as we have seen from the various experiential accounts of these different interviews, such construction can often make for a certain confusion and ambiguity.

To reiterate, this is of course only a partial reading and one which might also sound a little too functionalist. I am not suggesting that rave matters and appeals *only* because it serves some kind of reconstructive social function. But I do believe that its appeal can be partly explained in terms of the form and content of the 'world' into which it enables access and the fictions which it works to generate. This world and these stories fit our times. The stories of raving women are, I believe, particularly useful to a study of new, post-feminist femininities because these are stories which challenge, reject, disturb or simply trouble an established sexual order. They are stories about a safe, exciting, autonomous and warm existence outside, or beyond, the hold which has, in the past, tended to confine women to the home and to the heterosexual partnership. Now this is clearly not to imply that such stories or fictions are entirely peculiar to dance culture, that they are a complete reversal of, or a departure from wider fictions of femininity. Things are changing within our world generally. In sexual-political terms, new ways of being are coming to surround us. My argument is that contemporary dance cultures (precisely because – and like youth cultures more generally – these encourage a certain creativity, imagination and expressivity) allow for particularly clear expressions of such change.

Rave culture has, I am therefore arguing, been very significant within these changing social times. This is not only because like all youth cultures, it allows for a certain creativity but also because discursively, materially and practically rave is structured in such a way that aspects like safety, 'solidarity' and 'madness' are valued. It constitutes a space and a set of conditions which both speak our times and which allow for an assessment, exploration and statement on these times. When it comes to a breakdown of traditional fictions of femininity, rave culture has played its part in both 'causing trouble' and also, in providing some kind of symbolic resolution.

It is of course, impossible to speak of anything like a unidirectional flow of information when it comes to the relationship between rave culture and changing modes of femininity. Have (like many of the interviewees with whom I worked, claim) techno-dance cultures been somehow 'responsible' for the production of new ways of doing femininity? Has the heady world (of dance, music and ecstasy) which came to be called 'rave culture' simply revealed to young women new (and otherwise unlikely) experiential possibilities and interpersonal/intersexual organisations? Did British rave culture simply extend an invitation to previously uninvited guests; affording women entry into a 'safe', communal and 'positive' space in which it is possible to see oneself as 'mad', 'wild', 'adventurous' and so forth? This is in fact, what many of the present interviewees claimed. 'Rave changed sex roles for ever', argues Clare for instance. Miriam says, 'It's all down to rave. It's made an enormous difference between men and women.' Are these women right? Is this all about the advent of British Rave. Do other aspects of social life, other ideological shifts, other changes not matter? Is the development of feminism for example, not important? Or, has the breakdown of traditional sexual ideologies, the collapse of familiar fictions about femininity's 'rightful' life-course, and the many impacts of feminism been the real reason for the birth of the raving woman? Would the 'post-feminist' woman (precisely because she *is* more assertive, more independent, less tied to home, and because she is aware of living through a certain 'confusion') have gotten as much out of *any* kind of music scene? Does the specificity of the rave scene itself, actually matter at all?

Clearly, such distinctions are pointless. It is impossible to separate rave culture from its wider situation within a time and place wherein, among other things, femininity is undergoing a very obvious troubling. It is impossible that is, to imagine how things *might* have been differently. Contemporary social dance cultures and contemporary femininities are developing at the same time, in the same place. The coincidence is crucial and I do maintain that rave culture and changing femininities have mutually informed each other's development. Although it could be argued that rave and post-rave dance scenes would have been just as appealing, popular and enduring, had these not seemed in some way 'different' or challenging in sexual-political terms, I personally doubt it. For many men too – and as Jeremy Gilbert (1999) reminds us – much of rave's appeal is bound up with its provision of a space wherein both masculinity and femininity can be momentarily undone or disarticulated. And such an undoing says a lot about a wider time and place. If, for example, women are finding a new sense of 'home' within House – (if they have moved from an identification with enclosure and 'home' to one with adventure and excitement as they find these in House and techno-music cultures) – then this says a lot about the erosion of traditional senses of female belongingness. But it also says a lot about the development of a dance culture in which such an erosion can be publicly, safely, ecstatically and collectively addressed and worked out. If femininity is currently in a state of uncertainty, then rave and post-rave dance cultures can be seen to both express – even ritualise – this uncertainty (as in the frenzied incitement to 'lose it') and to throw up their own versions of a 'magical resolution'.

Bibliography

Adair, C. *Women and Dance: Sylphs and Syrens* (London: Macmillan, 1992).

Alcoff, L. and E. Potter (eds) *Feminist Epistemologies* (London: Routledge, 1993).

Ang, I. *Watching Dallas* (London: Routledge, 1985).

Ang, I. *Desperately Seeking the Audience* (London: Routledge, 1991).

Barthes, R. *Mythologies* (London: Paladin, 1972).

Baudrillard, J. *The Beaubourg Effect: Implosion and Deterrence in 'October 20'* (Spring, 1982).

Bey, H. *T.A.Z. The Temporary Autonomous Zone: Ontological Anarchy, Poetic Terrorism* (Brooklyn: Autonomedia, 1985).

Blum, L. 'The Discotheque and the Phenomenon of Alone-togetherness: a study of the young person's response to the Frug and comparable current dances' (*Adolescence* 1, 1966).

Boyne, R. and A. Rattansi. *Postmodernism and Society* (London: Macmillan, 1990).

Bradby, B. 'Sampling Sexuality: Gender, Technology and the Body in Dance Music' in *Popular Music* 12/2 (May 1993).

Braidotti, R. *Patterns of Dissonance* (Cambridge: Polity, 1991).

Braidotti, R. *Nomadic Subjects: Embodiment and Sexual Difference in Contemporary Feminist Theory* (New York: Colombia University Press, 1994).

Brennan, T. (ed.) *Between Feminism and Psychoanalysis* (London: Routledge, 1989).

Brunsdon, C. and D. Morley. *'Everyday Television "Nationwide"'* (London: British Film Institute, 1978).

Butler, J. *Gender Trouble: Gender and the Subversion of Identity* (New York: Routledge, 1990).

Butler, J. *Bodies that Matter: on the Discursive Limits of Sex* (New York: Routledge, 1993).

Chambers, I. *Popular Culture: the Metropolitan Experience* (London: Routledge, 1986).

Clifford, J. and G. Marcus (eds) *Writing Culture: the Poetics and Politics of Ethnography* (London: University of California Press, 1986).

Cosgrove, S. 'Against Health and Efficiency: Independent Music in the 1980s' in A. McRobbie, *Zoot Suits and Second Hand Dresses: an Anthology of Fashion and Music* (London: Macmillan, 1989).

Coward, R. *Female Desire: Women's Sexuality Today* (London: Paladin, 1984).

De Certeau, M. *The Practice of Everyday Life* (Berkeley: University of California Press, 1994).

Deleuze, G. and F. Guattari, *A Thousand Plateaus: Capitalism and Schizophrenia* (London: Athlone Press, 1988).

Diamond, I. and L. Quinby (eds) *Feminism and Foucault: Reflections on Resistance* (Massachusetts: Northeastern University Press, 1988).
Dreyfus, H. and P. Rabinow, *Michel Foucault: beyond Structuralism and Hermeneutics* (Chicago: University of Chicago Press, 1982).
During, S. (ed.) *The Cultural Studies Reader* (London: Routledge, 1993).
Dyer, R. 'In Defence of Disco', in S. Frith and A. Goodwin (eds) *On Record: Rock, Pop and the Written Word* (London: Routledge, 1990).
Fergusson, M. and P. Golding (eds) *Cultural Studies in Question* (London: Sage, 1997).
Foster, S. L. *Reading Dancing* (Berkeley: University of California Press, 1988).
Foucault, M. *The History of Sexuality* (London: Penguin, 1978).
Foucault, M. *Power/Knowledge: Selected Interviews and Other Writings 1972–1977*, ed. C. Gordon (New York: Pantheon Books, 1980).
Foucault, M. *The Care of the Self: the History of Sexuality*, Vol. 3 (London: Penguin, 1984).
Foucault, M. 'Technologies of the Self' in L. H. Martin, H. Gutman and R. H. Hutton (eds) *Technologies of the Self. Seminar with Michel Foucault* (London: Tavistock, 1988).
Frith, S. *Music for Pleasure* (London: Polity, 1988).
Frith, S. and A. Goodwin (eds) *On Record: Rock, Pop and the Written Word* (London: Routledge, 1990).
Gaines, J. and C. Herzog (eds), *Fabrications: Fashion and the Female Body* (London: Routledge, 1990).
Geertz, C. and G. E. Marcus (eds) *Writing Culture: the Poetics and Politics of Ethnography* (London: University of California Press, 1986).
Geraghty, C. *Raise your Hands* (London, Boxtree, 1996).
Gilbert, J. 'Dance Cultures and New Urban Oppositional Movements' (Paper Presented at *Signs of the Times* Conference, London: 1996).
Gilbert, J. and E. Pearson. *Discographies: Dance Music, Culture and the Politics of Sound* (London: Routledge, 1999).
Gilroy, P. *There Ain't no Black in the Union Jack* (London: Hutchinson, 1987).
Goodwin, A. 'Sample and Hold: Pop Music in the Age of Digital Reproduction' in S. Frith and A. Goodwin (eds) *On Record: Rock, Pop and the Written Word* (London: Routledge, 1990).
Gordon, C. (ed.) *Power/Knowledge: Selected Interviews and Other Writings by Michel Foucault* (New York: Pantheon, 1980).
Gotfrit, L. 'Women Dancing Back: Disruption and the Politics of Pleasure', *Journal of Education* 170/3, 1988.
Griffin, C. *Representations of Youth: the Study of Youth and Adolescence in Britain and America* (Cambridge: Polity, 1993).
Grossberg, L. 'Wandering Audiences, Nomadic Critics' in *Cultural Studies* (Issue 2, Vol. 3, October 1988).
Grossberg, L., C. Nelson and P. Treichler (eds) *Cultural Studies* (London: Routledge, 1992).
Grosz, E. *Volatile Bodies: towards a Corporeal Feminism* (Indianapolis: Indiana University Press, 1994).
Grosz, E. *Space, Time and Perversion* (New York: Routledge, 1995).

Hall, S. 'Introduction: Who Needs "Identity"?' in S. Hall and P. du Gay (eds) *Questions of Cultural Identity* (London, Sage, 1996).

Hall, S. and P. du Gay (eds) *Questions of Cultural Identity* (London, Sage, 1996).

Hall, S. and M. Jacques (eds) *New Times: the Changing Face of Politics in the 1990's* (London: Lawrence and Wishart, 1989).

Hall, S. and T. Jefferson (eds) *Resistance through Rituals: Youth Subcultures in Post-War Britain* (London: Harper Collins, 1976).

Hamment, D. 'Acid Warriors', Paper presented at *'Youth 2000' International Conference* (University of Teesside, Middlesbrough: July 1995).

Hamment, D. 'From Boomtown to Doomtown', Paper presented at *'Youth 2000' International Conference* (University of Teesside, Middlesbrough: July 1995).

Hanna, J. L. *Dance, Sex and Gender* (Chicago, University of Chicago Press, 1988).

Haraway, D. *Simians, Cyborgs and Women: the Reinvention of Nature* (London: Free Association Books, 1991).

Harris, D. *From Class Struggle to the Politics of Pleasure: the Effects of Gramscianism on Cultural Studies* (London: Routledge, 1992).

Hebdige, D. *Subculture: the Meaning of Style* (London: Methuen, 1979).

Heilbrun, C. G. *Writing a Woman's Life* (London: The Women's Press, 1989.

Henderson, S. *Ecstasy: Case Unsolved* (London: Harper Collins, 1997).

Hesmondhalgh, D. 'Dance Music Culture and Independent Record Companies since 1988' (Paper presented at post-graduate seminar, Goldsmiths College, March 1995).

Hesmondhalgh, D. 'The Cultural Politics of Dance Music' in *Soundings* (Issue 5, Spring 1997).

Hoggart, R. *The Uses of Literacy* (Harmondsworth: Penguin, 1957).

Hollway, W. *Subjectivity and Method in Psychology: Gender, Meaning and Science* (London: Sage, 1989).

Huq, R. 'Britpop' (Paper Presented at *Signs of the Times* Conference, London: 1996).

Hutcheon, L. *The Politics of Postmodernism* (London: Routledge, 1989).

Ingram, M. *Now We Are Thirty* (London: Methuen, 1982).

Irigaray, L. 'The Gesture in Psychoanalysis' in T. Brennan (ed.) *Between Feminism and Psychoanalysis* (London: Routledge, 1989).

Jordan, T. 'Collective Bodies: Raving and the Politics of Gilles Deleuze and Felix Guattari' in *Body and Society* (Issue 1, Vol. 1, March 1995).

Kamuf, P. (ed.) *A Derrida Reader: between the Blinds* (New York: Harvester Wheatsheaf, 1991).

Kohn, M. *Dope Girls: the Birth of the British Drug Underground* (London: Lawrence and Wishart, 1992).

Laclau, E. *New Reflections on the Revolutions of our Times* (London: Verso, 1990).

Laing, R. *The Nature of Dance: an Anthropological Perspective* (London: Macdonald and Evans, 1975).

Lash, S. and J. Urry. *Economies of Signs and Spaces* (London: Sage, 1994).

Lees, S. *Sugar and Spice: Sexuality and Adolescent Girls* (London: Penguin, 1993).

Leigh Foster, S. (ed.) *Corporealities: Dancing, Knowledge, Culture and Power* (London: Routledge, 1996).

Lipsitz, G. 'We Know What Time It Is: Race, Class and Youth in the Nineties' in A. Ross and T. Rose (eds) *Microphone Fiends: Youth Music and Youth Culture* (New York: Routledge, 1994).

Martin, L. H. and P. H. Hutton. *Technologies of the Self* (London: Tavistock Publications, 1988).

McClary, S. 'Same as It Ever Was' in A. Ross and T. Rose (eds) *Microphone Fiends: Youth Music and Youth Culture* (New York: Routledge, 1994).

McGuigan, J. *Cultural Populism* (London: Routledge, 1992).

McRobbie, A. *Zoot Suits and Second Hand Dresses: an Anthology of Fashion and Music* (London: Macmillan, 1989).

McRobbie, A. *Feminism and Youth Culture: from Jackie to Just Seventeen* (London: Macmillan, 1991).

McRobbie, A. 'Post-Marxism and Cultural Studies: a Post-script' in L. Grossberg, C. Nelson and P. Treichler (eds) *Cultural Studies* (London: Routledge, 1992).

McRobbie, A. 'Shut Up and Dance: Youth Culture and Changing Modes of Femininity' in A. McRobbie, *Postmodernism and Popular Culture* (London: Routledge, 1994).

McRobbie, A. (1997a) 'More! New Sexualities in Girls' and Women's Magazines' in A. McRobbie, *Back to Reality? Social Experience and Cultural Studies* (Manchester: Manchester University Press, 1997).

McRobbie, A. (1997b) 'Pecs and Penises: the Meaning of Girlie Culture' in *Soundings* Issue 5 (Spring 1997).

McRobbie, A. (1997c) 'The E's and the Anti-E's: New Questions for Feminism and Cultural Studies' in M. Fergusson and P. Golding (eds) *Cultural Studies in Question* (London: Sage, 1997).

McRobbie, A. *British Fashion Design: Rag Trade or Image Industry?* (London: Routledge, 1998).

McRobbie, A. *In the Culture Society: Art, Fashion and Popular Music* (London: Routledge, 1999).

McRobbie, A. and M. Nava, *Gender and Generation* (London: Macmillan, 1984).

Mellechi, A. 'The Ecstasy of Disappearance' in S. Redhead (ed.) *Rave Off: Politics and Deviance in Contemporary Youth Cultures* (Manchester: Manchester University Press, 1993).

Mitchell, J. and J. Rose. *Jack Lacan and the Ecole Freudienne: Feminine Sexuality* (London: Macmillan, 1982).

Modleski, T. *Loving with a Vengeance* (London: Methuen, 1984).

Morson, G. S. and C. Emerson. *Mikhail Bakhtin: Creation of a Prosaics* (California: Stanford University Press, 1990).

Muggleton, D. 'From Subculture to Neo-Tribe: Identity, Paradox and Post-modernism in "Alternative" Style' presented at *'Youth 2000' International Conference* (University of Teesside, Middlesbrough: July 1995).

Newcombe, R. *Rave and Dance Drugs: House Music Clubs and Parties in North-West England* (Liverpool: Liverpool Research Bureau, 1991).

Nicolson, L. (ed.) *The Second Wave: a Reader in Feminist Theory* (London: Routledge, 1997).

Penley, C. and A. Ross (eds) *Technoculture* (Minneapolis: University of Minnesota Press, 1991).

Penley, C. and A. Ross. 'Cyborgs at Large: Interview with Donna Haraway' in C. Penley and A. Ross (eds) *Technoculture* (Minneapolis: University of Minnesota Press, 1991).

Pini, M. 'Dance Classes: Dancing between Classifications' in *Feminism and Psychology* (Vol. 6, No. 3, August 1996).

Pini, M. (1997a) 'Women and the Early British Rave Scene' in A. McRobbie, *Back to Reality? Social Experience and Cultural Studies* (Manchester: Manchester University Press, 1997).

Pini, M. (1997b) 'Cyborgs, Nomads and the Raving Feminine' in H. Thomas (ed.) *Dance in the City* (Basingstoke: Macmillan, 1997).

Pini, M. 'Peak Practices: the Production and Regulation of Ecstatic Bodies' in J. Wood, *The Virtual Embodied: Presence, Practice, Technology* (London: Routledge, 1998).

Pini, M. 'Girls on "E": Social Problem or Social Panic?' in J. M. Ussher, *Women's Health: Contemporary International Perspectives* (London: BPS Books, 2000).

Pini, M. and T. Terranova. 'Intervista a Michelle Pole (Advance Party)' in A. Natella and S. Tinari (eds), *Rave Off* (Rome: Castellvechi, 1996).

Plumwood, V. *Feminism and the Mastery of Nature* (London: Routledge, 1993).

Probyn, E. *Sexing the Self: Gendered Positions in Cultural Studies* (London: Routledge, 1993).

Probyn, E. *Outside Belongings* (London: Routledge, 1996).

Rabinow, P. and W. M. Sullivan (eds) *Interpretive Social Science* (Berkeley: University of California Press, 1979).

Rabinow, P. (ed.) *The Foucault Reader* (London: Penguin, 1984).

Radway, J. *Reading the Romance* (London: Verso, 1984).

Redhead, S. *The End-of-the-Century Party* (Manchester: Manchester University Press, 1990).

Redhead, S. (ed.) *Rave Off: Politics and Deviance in Contemporary Youth Cultures* (Manchester: Manchester University Press, 1993).

Rietveld, H. 'Living the Dream' in S. Redhead (ed.) *Rave Off* (Manchester: Manchester University Press, 1993).

Rietveld, H. *This is Our House: House Music, Cultural Spaces and Technology* (Hants: Ashgate Publishing Ltd, 1998).

Roberts, R. *The Classic Slum* (Harmondsworth: Penguin, 1971).

Rolleston, J. 'The Politics of Quotation: Walter Benjamin's Arcade Project' in *P.M.L.A.* (July, 1989).

Rose, N. *Governing the Soul: the Shaping of the Private Self* (London: Routledge, 1989).

Ross, A. and T. Rose (eds) *Microphone Fiends: Youth Music and Youth Culture* (New York: Routledge, 1994).

Rumsey G. and H. Little. 'Women and Pop: a Series of Lost Encounters' in A. McRobbie, *Zoot Suits and Second Hand Dresses: an Anthology of Fashion and Music* (London: Macmillan, 1989).

Rust, F. *Dance in Society: an analysis of the relationship between the social dance and society in England from the Middle Ages to the present day* (London: Routledge and Kegan Paul, 1969).

Shotter, J. *The Cultural Politics of Everyday Life* (Buckingham: Open University Press, 1993).

Showalter, E. *Sexual Anarchy: Gender and Culture at the Fin de Siècle* (London: Virago, 1992).

Stanley, L. and S. Wise. *Breaking out Again: Feminist Ontology and Epistemology* (London: Routledge, 1983).

Straw, W. 'The Booth, the Floor and the Wall: Dance Music and the Fear of Falling', in *Public 8* (1993).

Strinati, D. *An Introduction to Theories of Popular Culture* (London: Routledge, 1995).

Sutcliffe, R. 'Techno Shamanism and Dance Cultures' (Paper presented at Goldsmiths College: March 1996).

Thomas, H. 'Movement, Modernism and Contemporary Culture: Issues for a Critical Sociology of Dance' (PhD thesis: London University, 1986).

Thomas, H. (ed.) *Dance, Gender, Culture* (London: Macmillan, 1993).

Thomas, H. (ed.) *Dance in the City* (Basingstoke: Macmillan, 1997).

Thornton, S. 'Strategies for Reconstructing the Popular Past' in *Popular Music* (Issue 9, Vol. 1: 1990).

Thornton, S. *Club Cultures: Music, Media and Subcultural Capital* (Cambridge: Polity, 1995).

Thrift, N. 'The Still Point: Resistance, Expressive Embodiment and Dance', Paper presented at *'New Cultural Studies' Conference* (Bristol University: July 1996).

Urry, J. *Consuming Places* (London: Routledge, 1995).

Walkerdine, V. *Schoolgirl Fictions* (London: Verso, 1990).

Walkerdine, V. *Daddy's Girl: Young Girls and Popular Culture* (London: Macmillan, 1997).

Walsh, E. *Ecstasy* (London: Minerva, 1996).

Ward, A. 'Dancing in the Dark: Rationalism and the Neglect of Social Dance' in Thomas, H. (ed.) *Dance, Gender, Culture* (London: Macmillan, 1993).

Waugh, P. *Feminine Fictions: Revisiting the Postmodern* (London: Routledge, 1989).

Weedon, C. *Feminist Practice and Poststructuralist Theory* (Oxford: Blackwell, 1987).

Wilkinson, H. *No Turning Back: Generations and the Genderquake* (London: Demos, 1994).

Wood, J. *The Virtual Embodied: Presence, Practice, Technology* (London: Routledge, 1998).

Index